Mythology

MYTHOLOGY

Jane Ellen Harrison

A Harbinger Book

HARCOURT, BRACE & WORLD, INC.
NEW YORK AND BURLINGAME

Library of Congress Catalog Card Number: 25-821

PRINTED IN THE UNITED STATES OF AMERICA

Contents

𝕓𝕓

Contents

Illustrations

Introduction

"We are all Greeks," says Shelley, in words thrice memorable, "our laws, our religion, our art, have their roots in Greece." True, but with one large deduction. Our religion is not rooted in Greece; it comes to us from the East, though upon it, too, the spirit of the West and of Greece itself has breathed. What Greece touches she transforms. Our religion, Oriental as it is in origin, owes to Greece a deep and lasting debt. To formulate this debt—this is the pleasant task that lies before us.

But first we must note clearly, our subject is not Greek and Roman religion but Greek and Roman mythology. Each and every religion contains two elements, Ritual and Mythology. We have first what a man *does* in relation to his religion, *i. e.*, his Ritual; then what he *thinks* and *imagines, i. e.*, his Mythology, or, if we prefer so to call it, his Theology. Both what he does and what he thinks are alike informed and vivified by what he feels, what he desires. Psychology teaches us—and here we cannot do better than quote Professor Leuba —that the unit of conscious life is neither thought, nor feeling, nor will, in separation, but "all three in movement towards an object." But it must further be noted that the will is primal. "Conscious life is always orientated towards something to be secured or avoided immediately or ultimately." Religion, then, is only one particular form of the activities of conscious life. The religious impulse is directed to one end and one only, the *conservation and promotion of life*. This end it attains in two ways, one negative, by the riddance of whatever is hostile, one positive, by the impulsion of whatever is favourable to life. All the world over, religious rites are of two kinds, of *ex*pulsion and *im*pulsion. Hunger and barrenness are the two first foes to man's life; these he seeks to expel. Food and fertility are his two primal goods. The Hebrew word for "good" meant primarily "good to eat." Food and fertility he seeks to *im*pel, to secure. Winter he drives out, spring and summer he brings in.

This primitive religious activity, these rites of expulsion and impulsion, this "will to live" in all its manifestations is world-wide; Greeks and Romans share it with Red Indians and South Sea Islanders. What then is it that is characteristically Greek or Roman? Wherein lies our debt? This brings us to the other side or phase or aspect of religion, to Mythology.

While man is carrying out his ritual, practising his rites of expulsion or impulsion, he is also thinking or imagining; some sort of image, however vague, rises up in his mind, some mental picture, some *imago* of what he is doing and feeling. Why does such an image arise? Here psychology steps in to help us.

Man is essentially an image-maker, but it is his human prerogative. In most animals, who act from what we call instinct, action follows on perception mechanically with almost chemical swiftness and certainty. In man the nervous system is more complicated, perception is not instantly transformed into reaction, there seems to be an interval for choice. It is just in this momentary pause between perception and reaction that our images, *i. e.*, our imaginations, our ideas, in fact our whole mental life, is built up. We do not immediately react, *i. e.*, we do not immediately get what we want, so we figure the want to ourselves, we create an image. If reaction were instant we should have no image, no representation, no art, no theology. The clearness, the vividness of the image will depend on the natural gifts of the image-maker. In one man's reaction the image will be dim, confused, non-arresting; in another it will be clear, vivid, forceful. It was the supreme genius of the Greeks as contrasted with the Romans that they were image-makers, *iconists*. In Greek mythology, we have enshrined the images fashioned by the most gifted people the world has ever seen, and these images are the outcome, the reflection of that people's unsatisfied desire.

Some decades ago it was usual to call Greek gods by Roman names. For Athena we said Minerva, for Eros Cupid, for Poseidon Neptune. This baleful custom is now happily dead. We now know that till they borrowed them from the Greeks the Romans never had in the strict sense of the word any *gods* at all. They had vague dæmonic beings, impersonal, ill defined, and these beings they called not *dei* (gods) but *numina* (powers). The Romans in the strict sense were never iconists, such was not the genius of their race; they did not personify, did not create personalities, hence they could not tell stories about persons, could not create *myths;* they had little or no mythology.

The Roman *numen* is devoid of human characteristics. He has not even sex, or at least his sex is indeterminate. How indefinite the *numen* is, is seen in the old prayer formula in which appeal is made to spirits, *sive mas sive femina* "whether he be male or female." These vague spirits or *numina* were associated with particular places and were regarded with vague feelings of awe inclining towards fear rather than love. The real specialization of the *numen* was not in his character but in his *function;* this area of action was carefully circumscribed; he presided over some particular locality and activity of man, and the *numina* were almost as numerous as the activities. Thus there is Cunina who guards the child's cradle, Edulia and Potina who teach him to eat and drink, Statilinus who makes him stand up and so on. In fact the *numen* is only the image of an activity, he is never a personality though he may be the first stage to impersonation.

If then the *numina* were superhuman, if they were in a sense lords over the Roman's life, if they inspired *religio*, awe and a sense of obligation, they were never human and of them there were no human-shaped, no anthropomorphic representations either in poetry or plastic art. Varro tells us —and we could have no better authority—that "for 170 years" (dating from the foundations of the city in 753 B.C.) "the Romans worshipped their gods without images." He adds—and the comment is curiously one-sided and thoroughly Roman: "those who introduced representation among the nations, took away fear and brought in falsehood." It was undeniably one supreme merit of the Greeks that from religion they took away fear. To the purely practical man the iconist is apt to seem a liar.

The Greeks themselves were in part conscious that they were iconists. One of the greatest of the sons of Greece has told us in simple words something of how the images were made and who were the image-makers. Herodotus has left us this statement, Herodotus who under the stimulus of foreign travel and especially a visit to Egypt had come to reflect on the characteristics of his own religion. He writes (II. 53):

But as to the origin of each particular god, whether they all existed from the beginning, what were their individual forms, the knowledge of these things is, so to speak, but of today and yesterday. For Homer and Hesiod are my seniors, I think, by some four hundred years and not more. And it is they who have composed for the Greeks the generations of the gods, and have given to the gods their titles and distinguished their several provinces and special powers and marked their forms.

Herodotus did not and could not know that the gods were the outcome, the utterance of human desire projected by rites of expulsion and impulsion. What he did know, thanks to his comparative studies, was that the Greek *gods* were a comparatively late product and that these personal, accomplished gods had been preceded by an earlier stage in which the gods were not in the Greek sense gods at all, not distinct personalities with characteristic attributes and life-histories, but shadowy, nameless powers more like the Latin *numina.* He knows of a race inhabiting Greece before Homer's days, and their gods, if gods they are to be called, are in marked contrast to those of Homer. "Formerly," he says, "the Pelasgians, on all occasions of sacrifice, called upon gods—but they gave them no title nor yet any name to any of them."

The primitive Pelasgians, equally with the more civilized Greeks, worshipped some form of divinity, they "offered sacrifice," they had ritual. But of what they sacrificed to, they had no clear conception. Their divinities were not individualized, they had not human forms, they were not called by proper names such as Zeus and Athena, they were not even addressed by descriptive titles such as the "Loud-Thunderer" or the "Grey-eyed One," they were more like Things or Powers than Persons. Comparative religion shows us that, as Herodotus first observed about the Greeks, so everywhere it is true that man only at a late stage attributes complete personality to the thing he worships. Personality comes with the giving of animal or human form. Before anthropomorphism (human form), before theriomorphism (beast form) we have a stage of animism when the gods are intangible forces dwelling anywhere and everywhere. They become real gods when man localizes them, gives them definite form and enters into fixed relations with them. Then only, when from Powers they become Persons, can they have a Mythology.

Into the causes that led to complete impersonation we shall not now enter. Some of them will appear in the course of our examination of the individual gods. What is important for the moment to note is that only when a god becomes a god in the full sense, *i.e.*, a Person, can a life-history, a *myth*, be made. Our business is with mythology. The Pelasgian divinities were impersonal, they had no myths; the same is true of the Roman *numina*. They were impersonal and had no myths. What is known as Roman mythology, the mythology, *e. g.*, of Ovid, is only Greek mythology transplanted and transformed into a Roman medium. Our debt to Roman mythology is soon acknowledged and promptly discharged, for it is practically *nil*. Roman mythology as contrasted with Roman ritual is non-existent. The Romans were deeply religious, deeply conscious of their obligation to the unseen; but they were not *iconists*, image-makers, mythologists, until late times and under Greek influence. The genius of their race forbade.

"The gods," says Herodotus, "were composed by Homer and Hesiod." The poets gave to them their titles, their special powers, their forms. To Herodotus Homer was a single person; to us Homer is the whole Epic tradition, the "traditional book" of the early Greeks, of a people of poets. The Greeks were not priest-ridden, they were poet-ridden, a people, as the word *poet* implies, of *makers, shapers*, artists. They started with the same religious material as other races, with fear of the unseen, with fetish worship, with unsatisfied desire, and out of this vague and crude material they fashioned their Immortals, such as Hermes, Poseidon, Demeter, Hera, Athena, Aphrodite, Artemis, Apollo, Dionysus, Zeus.

JANE ELLEN HARRISON

American Women's University Club,
4 rue de Chevreuse, Paris.

Mythology

I

Hermes

We shall begin with a lesser Olympian, with Hermes. Let us see him first with Homer's eyes. In the *Odyssey*, Zeus summons Hermes and bids him go to the island of Calypso:

> He spake: nor did the fleetfoot, Shining One
> Fail of obedience, but at once laced on
> Beneath his feet the imperishable fair
> Sandals of gold, that when he would be gone
>
> Over the wet sea or the boundless land
> Bore him like blowing wind, and took in hand
> The rod wherewith he charms men's eyes to sleep
> Or makes the sleeper to awake and stand:
>
> Holding it now, the Shining One with might
> Took wing, and mounting the Pierian height
> Out of the sky on ocean darted down
> And swift across the billows urged his flight
>
> As a sea-eagle that his finny prey
> Chases, his thickest plumage wet with spray,
> Through the dread gulfs of sea unharvested,
> Over the thronging waves he sped his way.[1]

Again and again Homer shows us the bright young messenger-god. He comes to rescue Odysseus from the fatal house of Circe and gives him the tragic herb *moly* to release him from her spells:

> So saying from the ship-side and the sea
> Inland I went alone, and presently
> Up the enchanted glades I drew anigh
> To the great house of Circe's sorcery.

> But, as I drew anigh it, in that place
> Gold-wanded Hermes met me face to face
> In likeness of a youth when the first down
> Fledges his lip in earliest manhood's grace;

. . . .

he utters his warning:

> So spake the Shining One, and forthwith drew
> Out of the earth that drug, and in my hand
> Laid it, and shewed me in what sort it grew.

> Black was the root, the blossom milky white
> And the gods call it moly: mortal wight
> Would have hard work to dig it from the ground;
> Howbeit the power of gods is infinite.[2]

Such is the Hermes we know, the Hermes worshipped by the later Greeks, the Hermes "composed" by Homer. A goodly *icon*, a fair image indeed! What were the materials that went to his fashioning?

The answer to this question is a surprise, almost a shock. It comes to us from the antiquarian Pausanias, who, in the second century A.D., travelled all over Greece and has left us his note-book. Happily he was a man for whom things ancient, even if uncouth and grotesque, had special charm. At Pharæ in Achæa, Pausanias (VII. 22. 2) saw an image of Hermes, the Market-God. It was of square shape, surmounted by a head with a beard. It was of no great size. In front of it was a hearth made of stone with bronze lamps clamped to it with lead. Beside it an oracle is established. He who would consult the oracle comes at evening, burns incense on the hearth, lights the lamps, lays a coin of the country on the altar to the right of the image and whispers his question into the ear of the god. Then he stops his ears and quits the market place, and when he is gone outside a little way, he uncovers his ears and whatever word he hears that he takes for an oracle.

Hermes was then, to begin with, what his name might lead us to expect, a *Herm*, a rude pillar later surmounted by a head (Fig. 1). But not only Hermes began life as a Herm, all the other gods it would seem had the like lowly parentage. At Pharæ, close to the image of Hermes, Pausanias goes on to tell us, stood about thirty square stones; these the people of Pharæ revered "giving to each stone the name of a god." And says Pausanias: "in the olden time all the Greeks worshipped unwrought stones instead of images." At Thespiæ he elsewhere (IX. 27. 1) notes the most ancient image of Eros, the winged love-god, was "an unwrought stone." At Orchomenus (IX. 38. 1) in Bœotia, where was a very ancient sanctuary of the Charites or Grace-Givers, their images were stones that had fallen from heaven.

The use of square-shaped images of Hermes, Pausanias in another part of his journal (IV. 33. 4) says was first introduced by the Athenians who were zealous in all religious matters, and from Athens the usage passed to the rest of Greece. How dear and how hallowed were these square-shaped Herms was clearly seen by the horror and panic that ran through Athens when at the time of the fatal Sicilian expedition the Hermæ were sacrilegiously mutilated. The

Arcadians, also a primitive people, were "specially fond" of the square-shaped Herm. At Megalopolis, Pausanias (VIII. 32. 3) saw images of the gods made in square form and called Workers. The contrast between the square Herms and the human-shaped Olympians evidently struck him, for he says: "Touching Hermes the poems of Homer have given currency to the report that he is the servant of Zeus and leads down to hell the souls of the departed."

We have seen Hermes in Homer as the messenger from heaven to earth; let us now see him as conductor of souls to Hades.

The wooers in the halls of Odysseus are slain, Hermes comes to lead their souls to Hades.

Now Cyllenian Hermes called forth from the halls the souls of the wooers, and he held in his hand his wand that is fair and golden, wherewith he lulls the eyes of men, of whomso he will, while others again he even wakens out of sleep. Herewith he roused and led the souls who followed gibbering. And even as bats flit gibbering in the secret place of a wondrous cave, when one has fallen down out of the rock from the cluster, and they cling each to each up aloft, even so the souls gibbered as they fared together, and Hermes, the helper, led them down the dank ways.[3]

Hermes is a square post, Hermes is a winged messenger. No contrast it would seem could be more complete, no functions more incompatible. The whole gist of the Herm is to remain steadfast, the characteristic of the messenger is swift motion. The Herm's modern brother, the Pillar-Box, would be quite useless but for the aid of half-a-dozen postmen. The Greeks themselves felt the anomaly, the incompatibility of the two figures; it must have tried the faith of many a simple worshipper. Babrius, writing in the 2d or 3rd century A.D.,

FIGURE 1 *Hermes as Herm*

in one of his fables makes the god himself voice the dilemma: was he a tombstone, was he an immortal?

> A stonemason made a marble Herm for sale
> And men came up to bid. One wanted it
> For a tombstone, since his son was lately dead.
> A craftsman wanted to set it up as a god.
> It was late, and the stonemason had not sold it yet.
> So he said, "Come early to-morrow and look at it again."
> He went to sleep and lo! in the gateway of dreams
> Hermes stood and said "My affairs now hang in the balance,
> Do make me one thing or another, dead man or god."

What then is the link that binds together Herm and winged messenger? How in a word did the Hermes of Homer come to be "composed" out of the square-shaped boundary stone?

Within the limits of Greece I might have asked the question and never found an answer. Happily the comparative method is at hand to help and it is Russia this time that brings the solution. The burial rite of the Eastern Slavs is thus described in an ancient Chronicle. After a sort of "wake" had been held over the dead man, the body was burnt and the ashes, gathered together in a small urn, were set up on a pillar or herm where the boundaries of two properties met. The dead grandfather was the object of special reverence under the title of *Tchur*, which means in Russian either grandfather or boundary. In the Russian of to-day *prashtchur* means great-great-grandfather and *Tchur menya* means "may my grand-father preserve me." On the other hand the offence of removing a legal landmark is expressed by the word *tchereztchur* which means "beyond the limit" or "beyond my grandfather." The grandfather looked after the patriarchal family during his life, he safeguarded its boundaries in death. His monument was at once tombstone and *Herm*.

Light begins to dawn. Hermes is at first just a Herm, a stone or pillar set up to commemorate the dead. Into that pillar the mourner outpours, "projects" all his sorrow for the dead protector, all his passionate hope that the ghost will protect him still. When in the autumn he sows his seed, he buries it in the ground as he buried his dead father or grandfather, and he believes that the dead man takes care of it, fosters it in the underworld and sends it up to blossom in spring and to fruit in autumn. So the Herm became the guardian of his buried wealth and Hermes is Charidotes, Giver of Grace or Increase of All Good Luck.

And more than this. In his lifetime a man went to his father or his grandfathers, to his elders for advice—surely they will not fail him now. So at night he steals to the Herm and asks his question. The Herm is dumb but the first chance word the man hears comes to him as an oracle from the dead. The dead are always magical, they can prevail where the living fail, so on the Herm he figures the *rhabdos* which is not a messenger's staff, not a king's sceptre but simply a magician's wand. And about it he coils snakes for he has seen a snake coiling about the tomb, creeping out of it, and a snake is the symbol of the dead man.

If the worshipper is an agriculturist his desire will be for his seeds and the Herm will be the guardian of his crops. But if he be a shepherd not less will he look to his dead ancestor to be the guardian of his sheep, to make them be fruitful and multiply. So when the Herm gets a head and gradually becomes wholly humanized, among a pastoral people he carries on his shoulders a ram, and from the Ram-Carrier, the Criophorus, Christianity has taken her Good Shepherd.

But it is not only the seeds and the flocks that the dead ancestor must watch over. More important still, he is guardian of the young men, the children of his clan. He is child-rearer, Kourotrophos. And finally when he is translated to Olympus he still watches over the infant gods, and Praxiteles so fashions his image—"Hermes carrying the child Dionysus."

How exactly the leap to Olympus was accomplished we do not know. At some time in Greek pre-history, owing to the movements of peoples and certainly before Homer, the Greek gods were assembled on the high peak of Mount Olympus in Thessaly, a peak that I have only seen shrouded in clouds. From the mountain peak to the sky transition was easy and natural. The old boundary-god, the steadfast Herm, had been the medium of communication with the ghosts below; it was natural he should be the messenger of the gods above, only he must shift his shape. His feet, once rooted in the ground, are freed and fitted with winged sandals, his magician's staff with its snakes he keeps, only now it has become a herald's staff—and he himself has shed his age and is a young man "with the first down upon his cheek."

It is as the messenger that modern art and literature remember Hermes, the messenger and herald,

New-lighted on a heaven-kissing hill.[4]

II

Poseidon

Hermes, beautiful, magical as he is, remains always a lesser, perhaps the least Olympian. We turn to another and a greater god, second only to Zeus himself, Poseidon. What were the thoughts, the longings, the ideals enshrined by the Greeks in the figure of Poseidon?

At first all seems simple and straightforward. Poseidon is the god of the sea, the sea incarnate. In Homer, as Professor Gilbert Murray says, Poseidon "moves in a kind of rolling splendour." Now as regards the other gods we have, too tardily, given up these simple, elemental interpretations. We no longer say that Athena is the Bright Sky or the Storm-Cloud, or that Hermes is the Whistling Wind. But Poseidon we are still apt to feel is in some special way "elemental." It is perhaps because, as Mr. Gladstone long ago pointed out, Poseidon is in Homer marked by an "absence of the higher elements of deity whether intellectual or moral." He is "a vast force and almost always a vindictive one." The real reason of this will appear later. It is certainly not because Poseidon is the sea. The sea that laps the isles of Greece is friendly rather than destructive.

If we would find the true answer we must ask the right

question. To-day we no longer ask *who was Poseidon?* All of us, even the most orthodox, agree that there never was, never could be, a god Poseidon. There were images of the god, but no god. But though no god Poseidon was, there were *worshippers of Poseidon,* people who imagined the god, who made images of him and who were themselves influenced by these images. A god is an *idolon,* an imagined potency, his worshippers are actualities. It is not the god who creates the worshippers. It is the worshippers who, in their own image, create, project the image of the god. "An honest god's the noblest work of man" remains the profoundest of parodies.

The question then we ask now-a-days is: Who and what were the worshippers of Poseidon? What was their environment? What—as the psychologists say—were their "reactions" to this environment? What their social activities, their means first and foremost of earning their bread, what their hopes, their fears, their desires, their aspirations, and how did these take shape in the figure of the god?

In thinking of Poseidon as sea-god we must never forget that the Greek attitude of mind towards the sea was not ours. To us the sea is the highway of trade, the means of abundant profit and sustenance. To the Greek it was always "the unharvested" sea, a barren salt waste where he might not plough or sow. It yielded, however, one form of sustenance, fish, and the later Greeks, unlike the Homeric heroes, were largely fish-eaters. Poseidon was not the sea incarnate, but he was the projection of the hopes and desires of a fisher-people. This is certain from his trident, which at least by some was understood as the fisherman's three-pronged spear. The Chorus in the *Seven against Thebes* (130) pray: "O thou Poseidon, steeded monarch who rules the sea with fish-spearing trident, grant release from our terrors," and on a black-figured lecythus Poseidon is figured sitting quietly on a rock, a fish in one hand, his trident in the other, while his friends Heracles and Hermes fish with other implements, line and basket.

The Chorus in the *Seven against Thebes* invoke "steeded Poseidon," Poseidon Hippius, God of the horses. It was Poseidon, Homer (*Il.*, XXIII. 276) tells us, who gave to Peleus his immortal horses. But our most important evidence is the express testimony of the Homeric *Hymn*—as follows:

Twofold, Shaker of the Earth, is the meed of honour the gods have allotted thee, to be the "Tamer of Horses" and the "Succour of Ships."

Here be it observed the horse-aspect even takes precedence over the sea aspect. Further, Pausanias (VII. 21. 9) tells us that Pamphus, who composed for the Athenians their most ancient hymns, says that Poseidon is

Giver of horses and of ships with spread sails.

In Athenian later literature two great hymns to Poseidon come instantly to mind, the chorus in Sophocles' *Œdipus at Colonus* and the hymn in the *Knights* of Aristophanes. In the *Knights*, Poseidon comes before Athena, for Poseidon was, as we shall later see, the god of the old aristocratic order. The Knights invoke first and foremost

Dread Poseidon the horseman's King,

and only second do they add,

Hail Athena, the warrior-Queen.[5]

In the *Œdipus at Colonus*, at Colonus close to Athens, it is

FIGURE 2 *Poseidon as Horse-god*

Athena and her olive tree who came first, but in the antistrophe we have:

Son of Kronos, Lord Poseidon, this our proudest is from thee
The strong horses, the young horses, the dominion of the sea.
First on Attic roads thy bridle tamed the steed for evermore;
And well swings at sea, a wonder in the rower's hand, the oar
Bounding after all the hundred Nereid feet that fly before.[6]

It may perhaps at this point occur to some one to urge: This is mere poetry, why make a difficulty of it? The galloping, rearing horses are but racing, crested waves. Do we not still speak of the "white horses"? The objection might have some validity if it were in poetry only that Poseidon was *Hippius*, Horseman, but it must be remembered that he is also so figured in art. On a fragment of 7th century B.C. Corinthian pottery (Fig. 2) he is represented actually riding on a horse. In his left hand are the reins, in his right an attribute wholly irrelevant to the horseman, the trident fishing-spear. Moreover sacrifices of horses were solemnly made to Poseidon. In Illyria, every ninth year, Festus[7] tells us, a yoke of four horses was sunk in the waters. And if Illyria seem a far cry, according to Pausanias (VIII. 7. 2) the Argives of old threw horses, bitted and bridled, into Dione in honour of Poseidon. Dione was a freshwater spring at a place called Genethlium in Argolis, so here there is no question of "white horses" and the galloping sea waves.

At Onchestus in Bœotia, remote from the sea, we find again Poseidon as Lord of horses. In the Homeric *Hymn to Apollo* (230) we are told how the god in his journeying came to Onchestus "the bright grove of Poseidon." What is the sea-god doing with a grove? "There the new broken colt takes breath again, weary though he be with dragging the goodly chariot: and to earth, skilled though he be, leaps down the charioteer and fares on foot, while the horses for a while rattle along the empty car with the reins on their necks, and. if the car be broken in the grove of trees, their masters tend them there, and tilt the car and let it lie. Such is the rite from of old and they pray to the King Poseidon while the chariot is the god's to keep."

Commentators have broken their heads in the attempt to fix the exact nature of the rite. The details are certainly not clear but this much is beyond question; we have a rite of horse- and chariot-driving sacred from early days to Poseidon. The title by which the god is addressed, King (*Anax*), marks its antiquity. Onchestus was a great religious centre in the time of Homer. Strabo (IX. 31. 412) tells us that the Amphictyonic Council usually assembled there, but in his days it was bare of trees. Poseidon's "bright grove" must have faded and fallen.

Poseidon then so far is fisherman and horseman. Strange and incompatible enough are the two functions, but a stranger fact still remains to be faced. He is not only fisherman and horseman; he is bull-man.

On a black-figured amphora in the museum at Würzburg (Fig. 3) we have Poseidon figured in curious guise. He, Lord of the "unharvested" sea, holds in his right hand, with singular irrelevance, a great blossoming bough and he is seated on a bull. His left hand grasps a fish and behind him vaguely unattached is his trident. The god has so many attributes he cannot hold them all. He is a bundle of incongruities. What has the bull-god to do with the sea and the trident? What relation has the salt sea fish to the blossoming bough? The mythologist of by-gone days was hard put to it for an explanation; he was driven into all sorts of holes and corners to fit in the pieces of the puzzle. Poseidon he said had a title, *Phytalmius*, He-of-the-Growth. Poseidon was the god of fresh water as well as of the sea and so on. We shall see in a mo-

FIGURE 3   *Poseidon as Bull-god*

Frieze 3. Poseidon as Bull-god.

ment that by the new method which views the god not as a
separate entity but as a projection of his worshippers no in-
genuity is needed, the riddle solves itself.

But first the Bull-aspect of Poseidon must be more clearly
established. A single vase-painting is not adequate. One of
Poseidon's standing epithets was *Taureus*. In Hesiod's *Shield*
(103) Heracles says to the young Iolaus: "Young man,
greatly in sooth doth the Father of Gods and men honour
thy head, yea and the Bull-God, the Earth-Shaker." The
scholiast after his kind suggests that the god is called *Taureus*
because the sea roars and bulls roar. His second thoughts are
happier. It is the Bœotian way he says to call the god *Taureus*
because bulls are sacrificed to Poseidon, specially at Onchestus.
Or, he adds, is it that Poseidon had a bull's head? One thing
is abundantly clear, the scholiast did not know.

The animal on which a god stands or rides or whose head
he wears is, it is now accepted, the primitive animal form
of the god. Poseidon then had once for his animal form a
horse and also it would seem a bull. The bull was in the fullest
sense his *vehicle*, his carrier. As the god has himself no
actuality, as there *is* no god, his worshippers choose something, some plant or animal or man to be the vehicle of their
desires, to represent the god they have projected. Now a bull
is often thus chosen by a people of agriculturists; he is a
splendid symbol and vehicle of that intense and vigorous life
they feel without and within them; so is the horse to a people
of horse-rearers. Later when the worshipper is less impressed
by the life around him, when he gains the mastery over these
strong, splendid animals and comes to trust only or mainly in
his own strong right arm, the godhead of the sacred animal
dwindles and the worshippers become shy of a bull-god or a
horse-god.

But in poetry the godhead of the animal lingers, and
especially the terror and the divinity of the Bull remains. It

lives on in the story of the death of Hippolytus. Theseus, the father of Hippolytus, is son of Poseidon and Poseidon has granted him the boon that thrice his prayer shall be granted. When Theseus curses the innocent Hippolytus he says:

>   and by Poseidon's breath
> He shall fall swiftly to the house of Death.

Hippolytus is driving his chariot by the seashore when the curse falls; he has reached Saronis Gulf:

>   Just there an angry sound,
> Slow swelling, like God's thunder underground,
> Broke on us, and we trembled. And the steeds
> Pricked their ears skyward, and threw back their heads.
> And wonder came on all men, and affright,
> Whence rose that awful voice. And swift our sight
> Turned seaward, down the salt and roaring sand.

A great crested wave rose and broke and swept towards the car of Hippolytus:

> Three lines of wave together raced, and, full
> In the white crest of them, a wild Sea-Bull
> Flung to the shore, a fell and marvellous Thing.
> The whole land held his voice, and answering
> Roared in each echo.

The horses maddened race along the sand. In vain Hippolytus tries to check and turn them,

>   For when he veered them round,
> And aimed their flying feet to grassy ground,
> In front uprose that Thing, and turned again
> The four great coursers, terror mad. But when
> Their blind rage drove them toward the rocky places,

Silent, and ever nearer to the traces,
It followed.[8]

A "great Sea-Bull"— There is no such thing. That portent
born of the sea, that edges in awful silence up to the chariot
is the god himself, the imagined terror, and the thunder marks
his divine Epiphany.

Poseidon then is fisherman-god, horse-god, bull-god. Finally
we must never forget that though he is not the sea-incarnate,
he is not elemental, he is *ruler* of the sea, *pontomedon* as the
Greeks called him, *thalassocrat* as we should say to-day.
These various and contradictory aspects so puzzling to the old
method of mythology are clear enough once we adopt the
new, once we *state the god in terms of his worshippers:*
Poseidon fisher-god, horse-god, god of the blossoming bough,
bull-god. Finally we must never forget that imagined *idolon*
of a people of fishermen, traders, horsemen, agriculturists,
bull-rearers, thalassocrats. Now all these functions we of the
Anglo-Saxon race combine ourselves, we are a fisher-people,
we are agriculturists, horse-rearers, breeders of fat-cattle,
thalassocrats. Poseidon, Hippius, Taureus, Pontomedon might
have been projected by ourselves.

But the question before us is, whether there was *in antiquity*
a people fishermen, agriculturists, horse-rearers, thalassocrats
who actually worshipped the bull. The word *thalassocrat*,
ruler of the sea, instantly reminds us that the Cretan Minos
was the first of the thalassocrats. His god was the Minotaur,
the Minos-Bull. *The god Poseidon is primarily and in essence
none other than the Cretan Minotaur.*

Observe we say "primarily." Ultimately Poseidon was very
much more and also a good deal less than the Minotaur. I
offer, not an equation but certain steps in an evolution. I
would guard my somewhat alarming statement carefully.
The Minotaur is *not* identical with Poseidon, rather he is the

point de repère about which the complex figure of Poseidon slowly crystallizes. Beginning as an island holy bull, worshipped by a population of fishermen, agriculturists, and herdsmen, he developed with his people. As Minotaur he spread his dominion across the islands and the sea to Greece proper. There, shedding his horns and hooves, he climbed at last to the snow-clad heights of Olympus. Where and when he got his new name of Poseidon, which in all probability means Lord of Moisture, we cannot certainly say.

Let us seek the Bull-God at home in Crete. The Minotaur is of all mythological figures most familiar, though so long misunderstood. The palace of Cnossus is full of the Holy Bull; his Horns of Consecration are everywhere, the whole palace is his Labyrinth. The Minotaur to us has become a cruel master, calling every seventh year for his toll of victims, Athenian youths and maidens. This is because his figure is presented to us distorted by Athenian chauvinism. But on the Cretan sealing, discovered by Sir Arthur Evans, the Minotaur is no monster to be slain. He is a King-God and he is seated on a primitive throne, the folding stool in use among the ancients. Just such a folding stool, made by Dædalus of Crete, was preserved as a monument of the ancient kings in the Erechtheum at Athens. The head of the monster is indistinct but of his divine Bull's tail curling up behind his throne there is no doubt. In front of him stands a worshipper in adoration. So is it always, to your own worshippers you are a god; to the conquerors of those worshippers, who project their own hate, you are a monster, a devil.

What precisely *was* the Minotaur? Fortunately we know from the evidence of countless vases exactly how he was figured. He was a man with a bull's head and bull's hooves. Now there is no such thing as a man, an actual living man with a bull's head and hooves. Is the Minotaur then a fancy monster or what is the reality behind? What is the Minotaur in terms of his worshippers? The answer is clear, certain, illuminating. The Minotaur *is* one of his own worshippers, a royal worshipper, wearing a ritual mask, a bull's head and horns, and possibly though not certainly, a bull's hide. In Egypt, Diodorus (I. 62) tells us it was the custom in the ruling house to put on the head the foreparts of lions, bulls and snakes as tokens of royal dominion. Sir Arthur Evans kindly tells me that the ritual form of the Minotaur, as bull-headed man, can, he believes, be traced right back to the hieroglyphs of Egypt. The Minotaur is but King Minos masking as a Bull. The object is, of course, that the royal functionary as representative of the whole state may get for it the force, the *mana* of the holy animal, that like Hannah his "horn may be exalted." As to this ritual actuality of the Minotaur it is sometimes objected that the Minotaur may be merely a phantastic hybrid form, like the man-headed bulls who are frequently figured on coins as river-gods. But, mark the difference. A bull with a man's face or bust is a mere fancy, pure mythology with no ritual counterpart. Sophocles so imagined the great river Acheloüs. He makes the maiden Deianira say:

> A river was my lover, him I mean
> Great Acheloüs, and in threefold form
> Wooed me and wooed again: a visible bull
> Sometimes, and sometimes a coiled gleaming snake,
> And sometimes partly man, a monstrous shape
> Bull-fronted, and adown his shaggy beard
> Fountains of clear spring water glistening flowed.[9]

Such a figure has no ritual counterpart in actual life. Bulls do not go about masquerading as men to win the *mana* of men. A beast's lack of "free motor images," as the psychologists say, restrains him alike from the follies of magic and the splendours of religion. He has "too much sense," *i.e.*, he is too closely bound by the experimental method. But a man with a bull's mask is *not* a fancy, it is a ritual reality. It *was* a ritual reality in the days of King Minos. It is to-day. A last survival of the custom may be seen among the Berkshire morris-dancers. The masqueraders no longer actually wear the Bull's head, but they carry it aloft on a pole.

At Ephesus the young men who poured out the wine at the festival of Poseidon were, Athenaeus (p. 425 e.) tells us, called *tauroi*, bulls. In the light of the bull-masqueraders the title becomes clear. The "asses' ears" of Midas rest on a folk-tale, accounting for a similar ritual, imperfectly understood. Midas is a priest-dynast like Minos but he presides over an ass-worshipping tribe. The folk-tale of the man with animal ears or horns is worldwide and has probably everywhere a ritual origin. The wearing of horns and animal ears was first misunderstood, then, often, moralized; it was turned into a penalty for some act of *hybris* of overweening pride and insolence, but the real original *hybris* lay in the worshipper's effort to gain the fertility of the animal which was worshipped.

The sign of kingship and the kingdom in Crete, the "mascot" as we should call it, was, it would seem, the bull, just as the mascot of the kingdom of Athens was the Golden Lamb. King Minos, Apollodorus (III. 1. 3) tells us, wished to obtain the kingdom; so he prayed that a bull should appear to him. To whom did he pray? Whence came the bull? He prayed to Poseidon and Poseidon sent him up from the deep a magnificent bull; so Minos got the kingdom. The coming of the bull from the depths of the sea is like the coming of the bull for the destruction of Hippolytus. It is so manifestly non-natural that it must be based on very ancient tradition.

The fabulous island of Atlantis described for us in the *Critias* of Plato has been, we think correctly, identified with

Crete. Crete after her great splendour sunk for generations into almost total obscurity. The island of Atlantis Plato tells belonged to Poseidon. When the gods divided up the world Poseidon received for his lot the island of Atlantis and he begat children and settled them in a certain part of the island. It is interesting to find that the bull-service of Poseidon described in the *Critias* has very close analogies to the bull-service of Minoan Crete. It is as follows: Poseidon, says Plato, gave laws to the first men of Atlantis and these laws they inscribed on pillars in the god's precinct and pledged themselves to their maintenance. It must never be forgotten that Minos was according to Greek tradition the first Lawgiver, and as Lawgiver he lived on, "uttering dooms" to the dead men in Hades.

The ritual of the pledge to maintain the laws was on this wise. There were certain bulls allowed to range free in the sanctuary of Poseidon. The Kings hunted these bulls without weapons, using staves and nooses. Again be it remembered, the bull hunts and bull fights of the Minoans appear on many a fresco and gem at Cnossus. When a bull was caught, it was led up to the column and its blood was shed over the inscription. The blood of the victim, mixed with wine, was then drunk and curses invoked on those who disobeyed the laws. The remarkable analogy here is not the mere sacrifice of the bull but the conjunction of bull and pillar in Atlantis and the conjunction of bull and pillar in Crete. On the frescoed shrines of Cnossus the holy pillar rises straight out of the "horns of consecration." On the famous *Hagia Triada Sarcophagus* we have indeed no direct certainty that the blood of the sacrificed bull is actually applied to the pillar but the close conjunction of the two, sacrificed bull and pillar, makes it highly probable. Anyhow our main point is clear. Plato could hardly have imagined a ritual so strange and complex.

It must be traditional and its origin is to be sought in the ritual of the bull-Poseidon in Crete.

The holy bull of Crete was the symbol, the surrogate of a greater power than himself. He had another name than that of Minotaur, he was also called Talos. Talos is most familiar to us as the brazen man who guarded Crete, circling round the island three times a day. Minos when he married Pasiphaë, the All-Shining One, received from Hephæstus, Apollodorus (I. 9. 1) tells us, the brazen man Talos as a wedding-gift. Hesychius says that Talos means the sun, and Apollodorus (I. 9. 26), when telling how the Argonauts came to Crete, says: "Talos was a brazen man but some say he was a bull." Talos only concerns us in so far as he was a bull, the animal vehicle of the sun and obviously but another name for the Minotaur, son of Asterion (the Spangled One) with his solar labyrinth. Talos appears on the coins of Crete sometimes in the form of a butting bull, sometimes as a man holding in his hand like the Minotaur a stone, the symbol of the sun. The sun connection of the Minos-bull and Poseidon is worth noting, for it will be remembered it was Poseidon who took vengeance on Odysseus for his outrage on the kine of the Sun-god.

We have tracked the bull-god home to Crete. The Minotaur, the Minos-Bull, stands to us henceforth for all the splendour of the Minoan civilization. Poseidon *Pontomedon* is Minos the thalassocrat. He stands for a culture that in Greece was pre-historic. This explains much. In Homer, Poseidon claims equality with Zeus. He is obliged to yield to his brother's supremacy but he is always a malcontent and often in open rebellion, persistently vindictive. He is connected always with the impious and outrageous giants; the Cyclopes, a godless race, are his children. In the *Odyssey*, we learn that these Cyclopes took no heed of Zeus. Odysseus ap-

peals for mercy and hospitality in the name of Zeus, god of
strangers, and the Cyclops makes answer:

> Belike a fool are you,
> O stranger, or from far away have come,
> Who bid me fear or shun what gods can do.

> For the Cyclopes heed of Zeus have none
> The Thunder-bearer nor of any one
> Of the high gods: too strong are we by far.

And when Odysseus has blinded the one eye of the Cyclops,
he says to him:

> Then to your father, Lord Poseidon, pray
> To heal you.[10]

It was this antipathy to Zeus and this aloofness from the
Olympian assembly that made Mr. Gladstone long ago in his
monumental *Juventus Mundi* divine that Poseidon was in
some sense a foreigner. Casting about for a maritime people
known to the Greeks he hit unhappily on the Phœnicians.
The Minoan civilization in his days lay buried deep and forgotten in Crete. Had Mr. Gladstone lived to-day, I doubt not
that he would have been the first to hail the Minotaur as
Poseidon's prototype.

It may be noted here that on the mainland Poseidon is often
and indeed almost always a beaten god. He contends with
Hera for Argos, with Helios for Corinth, with Zeus for
Ægina, with Dionysus for Naxos; he was forced to exchange
Delphi for Calaureia with Apollo, and Delos for Tænarum
with Leto. In all cases he was worsted; only at Athens, after
contending with Athena, the two disputants were reconciled,
though obviously Athena remained the real mistress. Poseidon

was worshipped by the old aristocracy but his salt sea well could not rival her olive tree. All these legends show clearly, what we know from archæological and other sources, that the Minoan civilization came to the mainland and prevailed for a time, but was ultimately overlaid and in part ousted by a purely Hellenic culture of Zeus-worshippers.

With the Minotaur, the Bull-God, we are on firm Cretan ground. But what about the horse-god? Were the thalasso-crats and bull breeders of Crete also horse rearers? The Cretans had horses and chariots, that is certain. In the early part of the late Minoan period, which synchronizes with the early part of the Eighteenth Dynasty in Egypt, the horse makes its appearance on Minoan monuments. It is represented together with the royal chariot on the clay tablets which form the Palace accounts, just as during the same period (*circ.* 1500 B.C.) it appears on the tombstones and late frescoes of Mycenæ. But, and this is a most important point, by a happy chance we know that the horse was *imported* into Crete. A curious seal-impression found at Cnossus shows us a one-masted vessel with rowers beneath a sort of awning. *On* the vessel, not as we now expect in the hold, but superimposed over the whole design, stands a magnificent horse. The super-position must, Sir Arthur Evans observes, be taken as a graphic mode and we have here a contemporary record of the first importation of horses to Crete. The date of the sealing is roughly 1500 B.C.

Further, most happily, the sealing informs us whence the horse came. This is of cardinal importance for the history of the development of the cult of the horse-Poseidon. The dress-ing of the horse's mane in a series of tufts corresponds with that of the horses found on the fresco of the *megaron* at Mycenæ and there the horses are coloured a deep bay and they have nose-bands. This is contrary to the normal European and Asiatic custom but is in accordance with *Libyan* practice. The horse on the Cretan sealing is a Libyan thoroughbred. His fountain-springing tail confirms his origin. An imported horse is not an indigenous horse. We never hear of Crete as "horse-rearing," like Argos or Thessaly. We have no evidence in Crete of a primitive horse-cult. King Minos does not wear a horse's head. Talos the Sun-God, when he races round the island, has no chariot and horses; he goes day by day on foot. "Look at the character of our country," says Cleinias, the Cnossian, to the Athenian in the *Laws* (625 D): "Crete is not like Thessaly, a large plain; and for this reason they have horses there, and we have runners on foot here; the inequality of the ground in our country is more adapted to going about on foot."

In the light of the Libyan horse we begin to understand the explicit statement of Herodotus (II. 50) that Poseidon came to the Greeks from the Libyans. "This god," he says, "they learned from the Libyans, for no people except the Libyans originally had the name of Poseidon and they have always worshipped him." Further Herodotus tells us that it was from the Libyans that the Greeks first learned to yoke four horses to their chariots. Poets projected these Libyan borrowings back into mythical days. In the fourth *Pythian Ode* of Pindar, Medea prophesies to the Minyan Jason of the colonization of Cyrene and she foretells the strange change that will come over the sea-faring colonists. They will plant cities where Zeus Ammon's shrine is builded and *"instead of short-finned dolphins they shall take to themselves fleet mares and reins, instead of oars shall they ply and speed the whirlwind-footed car."*

Apollonius Rhodius, in his *Argonautica* (IV. 1341 ff.), tells of an earlier meeting of the Minyans (*i.e.*, the men of Minyas) with the horse-Poseidon in Libya. He brings his Argonauts, it will be remembered, from Crete to Libya, which is indeed the nearest point of the African continent. The Argonauts are caught and miserably stranded in the shifting shallows of the Syrtes, and Peleus, one of their leaders, was well nigh desperate but "there came to the Minyans a wonder, passing strange. From out the sea there leapt landwards a monster Horse. Huge was he with mane flowing in the wind. Lightly with his hooves did he spurn the salt sea foam, matching the wind." Like the Bull of Hippolytus, the monster Horse was a portent, was in fact the Epiphany of the god himself. Peleus, we are told, was glad in his heart for he knew that Poseidon himself would lift the ship and let her go.

In Libya and in Libya only does there seem a simple and natural reason why a sea-faring god should become a horse-god, because in Libya we have the steady tradition of a race of horses which were the wonder of the ancient world. The story of Pegasus, the winged horse, took its rise in Libya and hence must have been transplanted by Poseidon worshippers to Greece. The Mænads in the *Bacchæ* (990) sing that Pentheus is born of a lioness-mother of the race of the *Libyan* Gorgons. The *Kibisis* or leather wallet in which Perseus carries the severed head of Medusa is just the primitive bag in which the Libyan carried the stones which were his principal weapons. "The Libyans," says Diodorus (III. 49. 4), "go out to face the foe, armed with three lances and with stones in leather bags. They wear neither sword nor helmet nor any other weapon but look to get the better of their foe by swift movement. Hence they are very skilled in running and stone slaying." On a Corinthian vase Perseus is figured attacking the monster with stones. Andromeda by his side keeps him supplied from a goodly pile. Always in representations of the slaying of Medusa Perseus is hurrying along at a pace truly Libyan. On the shield of Achilles,

> All round the level rim thereof
> Perseus on winged feet above
> The long seas hied him.
> The Gorgon's wild and bleeding hair
> He lifted: and a herald fair
> He of the wilds whom Maia bare
> God's Hermes flew beside him.[11]

Horse and man alike were swift in Libya; the winged Pegasus is the counterpart of the winged Perseus.

Medusa, the mother of Pegasus by Poseidon, is generally credited with human shape. From her severed neck springs up the winged Pegasus, as on a white lecythus in New York City. But on one monument, a Bœotian stamped amphora in the Louvre, Medusa herself has the body of a horse, though the face of a woman. She is a horse-goddess and as such the fitting bride of the horse-Poseidon. The Bœotian horse-Medusa recalls the horse-headed Demeter worshipped at Phigaleia in Arcadia.

Before leaving the horse, one curious and interesting point must be noted. It has been already observed that, as contrasted with the bull, the horse had but small place in the ritual of Poseidon. But sometimes a ritual motive lurks concealed where least suspected. Such is, I think, the case with the famous Trojan Horse. The story of the horse, it has been thought, arose from a real historical incident misunderstood. The device of Epeius, the horsemaker, was really, it is said, the building of a wooden siege tower as high as the walls, with a projecting and revolving neck. Such an engine is figured on Assyrian monuments. But when we read the chorus of the *Trojan Women*, in which Euripides describes the Horse, it is impossible to avoid the conclusion or at least the suggestion that ritual rather than historic incident lies behind. The Horse is a "hobby-horse," a fertility horse, a thing that survives in village tradition and custom to-day. It was a dæmonic, even a divine thing. It was explained as a votive offering, when its real magical meaning was misunderstood. It was connected with a definite date in the calendar, with the setting of the Pleiades, always to the Greeks a season of agricultural importance; and above all it was brought up to the city in a great festal procession of young and old flute players and dancers, a regular Comus.

In the chorus of Euripides, the *Trojan Women* sing of it:

> A towering Steed of golden rein—
> O gold without, dark steel within
> Ramped in our gates: and all the plain
> Lay silent where the Greeks had been,

and again,

> O, swift were all in Troy that day,
> And girt them to the portal-way,
> Marvelling at that mountain Thing
> Smooth-carven where the Argives lay,
> And wrath, and Ilion's vanquishing:
> Meet gift for her that spareth not,
> Heaven's yokeless Rider;

and a maiden sings:

> I was among the dancers there
> To Artemis, and glorying sang
> Her of the Hills, the Maid most fair,
> Daughter of Zeus: and, lo, there rang
> A shout out of the dark, and fell
> Deathlike from street to street and made
> A silence in the citadel.[12]

In the Prologue to the same play Poseidon himself tells how

> The Greek Epeios came, of Phocian seed,
> And wrought by Pallas' mysteries a Steed
> Marvellous, big with arms: and through my wall
> It passed, a death-fraught image magical.

In "horse-rearing Argos" some hobby-horse must have formed part of a fertility ritual. The essence of the modern and apparently of the ancient hobby-horse was that it concealed actual live men. This ritual contrivance may actually have been used for some military ambush—but it is more likely that when its real ritual meaning was obscured it was misinterpreted. It is worth noting that the Trojan Horse has an odd Cretan counterpart which seems to have passed unobserved. Apollodorus (III. 1. 4) tells us that Dædalus to please Ariadne made a wooden cow on wheels, hollowed it out inside, flayed a cow, sewed the hide about his handiwork and put Pasiphaë inside. A wooden cow, a wooden horse, both hollowed to hold human beings. Both were part of some ritual gear of a magical "sacred marriage" or a ritual of resurrection. The tale of the Trojan Horse has all the air of a ritual fossil embedded. There could be no finer instance of the magic of Greek inauguration than the use Euripides has made of it in the Chorus of the *Trojan Women*. The uncouth even ugly contrivance is transmuted to a thing of wonder and beauty.

We have seen the Bull-God in Crete as thalassocratic, we have seen him become in Libya a Horse-God. We have now to watch him pass to the mainland to Greece proper. The cult of Poseidon occurs naturally in the bays and on the promontories of the coast line of Greece. We say "naturally," but if I am right the naturalness is not at all what it would seem at

first sight. The cult of Poseidon occurs in bays and on promontories not because it is a sea-cult but because those bays and
those promontories were the first landing places of the Minos-
Bull from Crete.

The bull of Minos waxed fat and kicked. King Minos desired not only what was his natural right, the hegemony of
the Ægean islands. His lust for empire was his undoing. But
at first all went well. During the third and second millenniums
B.C., the Cretans colonized Greece. *The sites of Poseidon-
worship are the landing places of immigrant Minoans.* Into
the archæological evidence of this we cannot here enter. It is
enough to state the simple fact that *at each and every site of
Poseidon worship on the mainland, Mycenæan (i.e., late-
Minoan) antiquities have come to light.*

Let us take an instance.

In the *Odyssey*, Telemachus reaches Pylus on the coast of
the western Peloponnese. What does he find at the " 'stab-
lished castle of Neleus" where dwells old Nestor "tamer of
horses"? Down on the sea shore the people

> Made to the blue-haired Shaker of the Earth
> Oblation, slaying coal-black bulls to him.
>
> Nine messes were there, and in each of these
> Five-hundred men set after their degrees
> Offered nine bulls: and then on the inward meat
> They fed and burned to God the thigh-pieces.
>
> .   .   .
>
> And to Poseidon the Protector now
> Made supplication, saying, "Hearken thou,
> Poseidon, Girdler of the Earth, nor grudge
> Our work to end according to our vow." [13]

The site of the modern Kakovàtos, shown by Professor Dörp-
feld to be the Homeric Pylus, has yielded the beehive tombs
which their contents show to be as early as late Minoan II.

Going Eastward from Pylus we come to Tænarum. This
great promontory was probably one of the first points at
which the immigrant Minoans would touch. Nor is this contact mere conjecture. Plutarch (*De sera numinis vindicta,* 17)
tells us of a certain man who had slain Archilochus and was
bidden by the Pythian priestess to go to appease the ghost—
to the "habitation of Tettix." The "habitation of Tettix" Plutarch explains was Tænarum, for there, they said, Tettix the
Cretan came with a fleet. The name Tettix "cicada" smacks
of things ancient. Pindar too remembers Tænarum (*Pyth.,*
IV. 75) and connects it with Euphemus son of Poseidon. The
Poseidon cult at Tænarum, it is important to note, was mainly
in the hands of a subject race, the Helots. Poseidon was worshipped there as Asphaleius, which means not the steadfast
earth but the safe asylum. Poseidon to the oppressed Helots
was a veritable Rock of Ages. In the rocks of Tænarum were
found seventy bronze statuettes representing bulls and horses.
Here too were found inscriptions dedicating slaves to the service of Poseidon.

By each one of the great sea gates, the gulfs of Messene, of
Laconia, of Argolis, and by the Saronic gulf and the channel
of the Euripus, Minoan settlers entered Greece, but nowhere
did they leave more manifest mark than in Argolis. The
plain of Argos was and is still rich and "horse-breeding"
though the harbourage is bad. It may be for that reason that
the Minoan fortresses are all planted inland. Palamedes
brought the Cretan script to the sea-town of Nauplia but
Tiryns with its citadel is two miles inland. We have seen that
at Dione horses were offered to Poseidon. It is natural to ask
have we also traces of the bull-god? Fortunately yes. The

frescoes of Tiryns with their bull-fights take us straight back to Crete; they might have adorned the palace of King Minos. Moreover an odd story in Athenæus (VI. 79) lets out that the regular offering to Poseidon at Tiryns was a bull. We do not think of the Tirynthians as a specially humorous folk but Theophrastus in his treatise on Comedy said they loved laughter and were quite unfit for serious business. They wished to cure themselves of this defect and consulted the oracle at Delphi. The god made answer that *when they were sacrificing a bull to Poseidon*, if they would throw it into the sea without laughing they would be cured. Very prudently they forbade the boys of Tiryns to come to the sacrifice but a boy got in among the crowd and when they tried to hoot him out he said "Yr'r frightened lest I should upset yr bull," and they laughed, and realized that the god had meant to show them it was impossible to uproot an old habit. The bull-sacrifices of Poseidon in Homer are things of tremendous solemnity, but here we get a glimpse of the lighter side of the matter.

Oddly enough Athenæus follows the story up by telling us, on the authority of Sosicrates in the first book of his *History of Crete*, that the people of Phæstus in Crete had the like reputation for lightheartedness. "The Phæstians," he says, "from earliest childhood practised the art of saying ridiculous things and the Cretans unanimously attributed to them pre-eminence in the art of raising a laugh." It is possible, nay probable, that these laughter-loving Phæstians crossed over from Crete to Tiryns. At Mycenæ we have no record of Poseidon cult; it was perhaps the most completely Achæanized of all the Minoan settlements, but the walls of Mycenæ, it was fabled, were built by the Cyclopes, children of Poseidon. Poseidon we know had once ruled over the whole land; he had shown the watersprings of Lerna to his bride Amymone and when the sovereignty of the land was adjudged to Hera, Poseidon in wrath dried up the springs and made Argos "very thirsty." The rival cult of Hera Boōpis (the Ox-faced) was rich in bulls, Argos himself Apollodorus (II. 1. 2) tells us wore a bull's hide and has strange analogies with the Minotaur. When the two bulls met it may well be that the bull aspect of Poseidon was obscured and that he wisely, in "horse-rearing Argos," specialized in horses.

Passing the great sanctuary of Poseidon on the island of Calaureia we come on the opposite mainland to Trœzen, associated always with the legend of Theseus. Trœzen, Strabo (VIII. 14. 373) says, was sacred to Poseidon and was once called Poseidonia. Plutarch (*Vita Thesei*, 6) tells us that the Trœzenians honoured Poseidon conspicuously, gave him the title of Poliouchus (Holder of the City), offered to him their first fruits and had his trident impressed on their coins. At Trœzen clearly Poseidon is much more than sea-god. Excavations on the site yielded a pre-historic pit-grave containing four large vases of "Mycenæan," *i.e.*, late Minoan, style. Trœzen had, like Athens, its legend of a contest between Poseidon and Athena for the land. Which legend is the prototype of the other is hard to say. In any case the moral is the same as in the case of Hera at Argos. We have an indigenous goddess of the land, a local Korè or Maiden and an immigrant god who strives with but partial success for the upper hand. Trœzen is not without its legend of Cretan immigration. The Trœzenians, Pausanias (II. 32. 2) says, honoured Damia and Auxesia and they said that these goddesses were *maidens who came from Crete*.

But the legend most important for our argument looks the reverse way and tells of the conquering expedition of a Trœzenian hero against Crete. And that hero is none other than Theseus.

Theseus, hero of Trœzen, is for our purpose a figure of the first importance. He is son of the local princess Aithra but his father is none other than Poseidon himself. Poseidon the story said met and loved the princess in the little island of Sphaira, close to Calaureia. Theseus stands for the blend of indigenous Hellene and immigrant Minoan. He also stands for the Amphictyony of Calaureia, potent in those early days and which linked up the coast cities from the promontory of Trœzen to Athens. He goes to Athens and stands also for the time when Athens held the hegemony of the coast confederation. His first work on coming to manhood is to cleanse the coast road of robbers, many of them sons of Poseidon like himself. By cleansing the road he makes the league of coast towns a possibility. All the mythology of Procrustes, Sciron, Sinis and the like, translated into pre-history, figure forth the league's great civilizing work. Calaureia stands for the dawning thalassocracy of the mainland, soon to meet Crete in mortal conflict.

The crisis is at hand. No sooner has Theseus reached Athens and been acknowledged heir of Ægeus than he is straightway sent off to Crete with the fatal tribute to the Minotaur. The Bull of Crete, that is Minos himself, has wasted Attica and subdued Megara and has been hardly bought off. The tribute-ship is matter of history. It was preserved by the Athenians down to the time of Demetrius Phalerius and was then so pieced and mended Plutarch tells us in his *Life of Theseus* that it afforded the philosophers an illustration in their disputations as to the identity of things changed by growth. In the days of Socrates the ship sailed for Delos but all men knew that in olden times the same ship had sailed to Crete with the tribute for the Minotaur. Owing to the Dorian conquest the religious centre had shifted from Crete to Delos. Poseidon had emigrated. In the current legend the two centres are awkwardly linked together. Theseus is made to call at Delos on his way home in order to dance the crane dance. It is rarely that we see pre-history so clearly reflected in mythology.

And finally, in the Labyrinth, Theseus slays the Minotaur. He, the son of Poseidon, he, who, according to another legend, married the Cretan Phædra and sent the bull of his father Poseidon to slay his son Hippolytus, he, Theseus, sails to Crete and slays the royal bull and drags him from his great palace. It all sounds at first paradoxical but viewing the god and the hero in terms of the worshipper the riddle is not hard to read. Theseus we must always remember is not Poseidon himself, only the son of, that is, the descendant of Poseidon. He stands, I think, for the worshippers of Poseidon partially Hellenized, Achæanized on the mainland. The bull of Cnossus had indeed waxed fat and kicked, imposing intolerable tribute on Athens, on Megara and probably on all the coast towns of the Amphictyony. The tributaries turned at last and some-where about 1400 B.C., Cnossus fell by the hands of her own children, the colonists of the mainland. The fall of Cnossus caused no breach in Minoan civilization: there was no in-trusion of an alien race.

Cnossus falls, the Minotaur is slain by the young Athenian hero Theseus, and henceforth for Athens and for all the civilized world that lay under the ban of Athens, the royal bull is a savage monster. *Væ Victis!* But Plato or whoever is the writer of the *Minos* (318 E) knew quite well that this was only because events were seen through hostile Athenian eyes. Crete was the mother and source not of barbarism, though her wealth is not wholly free from some tinge of barbaric excess, but of civilization. Minos to his enemies might be the "baleful one" but he was a mighty lawgiver and made piracy to cease. When in the dialogue the companion of Socrates ad-mits that Rhadamanthus was reputed a just judge, but would maintain that Minos was fierce and hard, Socrates turns on him and says, "but my good man you know that is but an Attic fable that you are telling, a stage-plot," and he himself tells a different tale. Even on Attic vase-paintings there are

traces of the sanctity of the Cretan Bull. He wears fillets like
the Minotaur. Commentators explain that he wears them "pro-
leptically" by anticipation, because he is about to be sacrificed
by Heracles or Theseus. He wears them, because he always
wore them, because he is the holy and royal Bull of Crete.

We have traced Poseidon from Pylus to Athens. It would
be easy and pleasant to follow his track further along the
coast round Attica by Bœotia through the Euripus by Eubœa
on to Iolcus and finally to Tempe. But space does not allow
nor is it needful for our argument. Everywhere we should
only find the same tale repeated, the worship of the bull-god
and the horse-god, the presence of the Minoans, the people
of Minos, and everywhere, when excavation has been made,
Minoan remains. Once Tempe reached, the Minoan colonists
seem to have paused; we find no more Minoan remains; the
horse-god and the bull-god disappear.

Poseidon has been dealt with at some length and at the
outset not because he is the most interesting of the Olympians
nor yet because he is the most characteristically Greek. Far
from it. He has been the subject of no great masterpiece of
art whether in poetry or sculpture. He has been chosen for
two reasons. First because he stands for that great pre-Hel-
lenic Minoan civilization without a knowledge of which it is
impossible nowadays to attempt any study of Greek art. The
Minoans were great civilizers, great artificers, great craftsmen,
and a people profoundly religious; they were not a people of
artists; with all their skill and all their splendid material and
costly apparatus they lack that instinct for beauty, that austere
reserve, that divine spark which was all Hellenic. We must
not ask of Poseidon what is not his to give. Secondly, Poseidon has been chosen because perhaps better than any other
god he illustrates the principle by which the new psychology

works, the principle namely that regards mythology and theology as springing, not clean and clear from man's imagination, but rather from man's, from the worshipper's reactions to his environment. There *are*, we repeat, no ancient gods; there *are* ancient reactions, emotions, activities, embodied in representations. It is for us to discover those reactions. In a word, mythology is *pre*-history and when it is confirmed by archæology, as in the case of Poseidon, we may venture to trust it.

III

卍卍卍卍卍卍卍卍卍卍卍卍卍卍卍卍卍卍卍卍卍卍卍卍卍卍卍卍卍卍卍卍卍卍

The Mountain-Mother

We have left behind us the figure of Poseidon but we have not yet done with Crete. Crete has given us a mythological figure of the first importance, the Mountain-Mother. On the clay impression of a signet ring (Fig. 4), found in the palace of Cnossus, she stands before us and this sealing is a veritable little manual of early Cretan ritual and mythology. When by the kindness of the discoverer, Sir Arthur Evans, I first saw its fragments in the Museum at Candia it seemed to me almost "too good to be true." On the summit of her own great mountains stands the Mother with sceptre outstretched. The Minoan women have indeed made their goddess in their own image. They have dressed her, wild creature though she was, as they dressed themselves in grotesque fashion in a flounced skirt, she has their narrow pinched waist and for solemn guardians they have given the fierce, mountain-ranging lions, placed heraldically to either side. These lions are thrice familiar. They guard the gate at Mycenæ, only there the goddess is figured by the pillar between them, here she has come to life, imperious, dominant. To the left of the goddess is a Minoan shrine with "horns of consecration" and pillars, the symbols that connect her with plant and animal life, for the

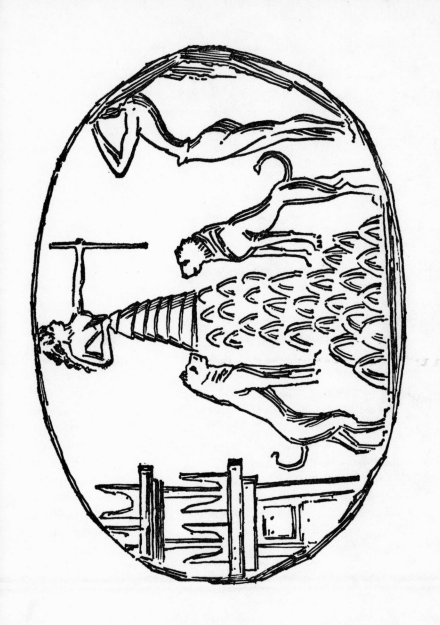

FIGURE 4 *The Mountain-Mother*

pillar is but tree shaped and stylized. Before the goddess stands a worshipper in ecstasy.

On this sealing the Mother, the Woman-Goddess, stands and rules alone. On other gems a male divinity descending from the sky sometimes appears. But always noticeably he is young and subordinate. In Minoan religion the male divinity is sometimes merely the attribute of motherhood, a child, sometimes a young man and sometimes a sky-power that fertilizes the Earth. Now this supremacy of the Mother marks a contrast with the Olympian system, where Zeus the Father reigns supreme. It stands for the Earth Worship as contrasted with the Sky. At Dodona the litany chanted by the priestesses has been preserved for us by Pausanias (X. 12. 10). It was as follows:

Earth sends up fruits, so praise we Earth, the Mother.

The mountain naturally enough in Crete stood for Earth, and the Earth is Mother because she gives life to plants, to animals, to man. When in the Eumenides of Æschylus the priestess of Delphi begins her address to the successive divinities of the place her opening words are:

First in my prayer before all other gods
I call on Earth, primæval prophetess.

Our modern patriarchal society focuses its religious anthropomorphism on the Father and the Son: the Roman Church with her wider humanity includes the figure of the Mother, who is both Mother and Maid. In this she follows the teaching of the Minoans. The mother and the father cults are in fact of supreme importance for our understanding of that complex structure Greek theology: they are characteristic of the two main strata that underlie Greek religion, the southern and earlier stratum, which is Anatolian as well as Cretan and has

the dominant Mother-God, while the northern stratum which
is Indo-European has the Father-God, head of a patriarchal
family and, ostensibly at least, in spite of countless amours the
husband of one wife. The northern religion of course reflects
a patrilinear, the southern a matrilinear social structure. It is
not a little remarkable and shows how deep seated was the
sense of difference that the Mother was never admitted to the
Olympus of Homer. Even Demeter, honoured though she
was through the length and breadth of Greece, had never in
Olympus any but the most precarious footing. In later, post-
Homeric days, when North and South were fused, a place
was found for the Mother in a more elastic Pantheon, as
Mother of the Gods.

The Homeric patriarchal Olympus reflected and was the
outcome of a "heroic" state of society, that is, it emphasized
rather the individual than the group, it resulted from warlike
and migratory conditions. On the other hand the worship of
the Mother emphasizes the group, the race and its continuance;
rather than the prowess of the individual, it focuses on the
facts of fertility and the fostering of life. Accordingly, she
being concerned with the group rather than the individual is
attended not only by her subordinate son and lover but by
groups of dæmonic persons, Curetes, Telchines, Corybantes,
Satyrs and the like. Of these we shall hear more when we
come to the figure of Dionysus the Son-God, but it must be
noted that these bands of worshippers also attend the Mother.
The chorus of Mænads in the *Bacchæ* of Euripides know that
their worship was one with the worship of the Mother—they
sing:

> But the Timbrel, the Timbrel was another's,
>   And away to Mother Rhea it must wend;
> And to our holy singing from the Mother's
>   The mad Satyrs carried it, to blend
>   In the dancing and the cheer

Of our third, and perfect Year;
And it serves Dionysus in the end! [14]

Another all-important point. The worship of the Mother
is always mystical and orgiastic. The mysteries of Greece
never centre round Zeus the Father, but rather round the
Mother and the subordinate son. The Olympian father and indeed all Olympian gods are approached in rational, anthropomorphic fashion; they are treated as magnified men addressed
by prayer, praise, presents—but the Mother is approached
by means that are magical and mysterious, she has mysteries.
Mysteries we no longer regard as mysterious in the sense of
unintelligible. They are simply magical rites, dramatic representations of birth, marriage and death, and they are per-
formed with the magical intent of promoting fertility. The
divinities who preside over these magical rites are always
vaguer in outline than those who are approached by prayer
and praise. The Mother was never so clearly and fully projected into human form as the Father. The mystery *par ex-
cellence* of the Mother was her "sacred marriage," a magical
ceremony for the induction of fertility.

The great Mother of Crete though she was never admitted
to Olympus had great influence on Greek thought and religion. Many of her sacred animals and attributes, much of
her nature in general, she lent to the women divinities of the
mainland. To Hera she lent her "sacred marriage," to Demeter her mysteries, to Athena her snakes, to Aphrodite her
doves, to Artemis all her functions as "Lady of the Wild
Things." And most of all the functions of the dominant goddess with the subordinate figure of the male attendant, half-
son, half-lover. Attis and Adonis are echoed again and again
in Greek mythology in those figures of Hera and Jason,
Athena and Theseus. Their high companionship does not
reflect the purely Greek relations of man to woman.

One lovely figure in Greek mythology undoubtedly comes straight to us from the Cretan Mother, that is the figure of Pandora, the All-Giver. On vase-paintings the Earth-Mother is often figured rising half out of the actual ground. On a red-figured amphora in the Ashmolean Museum at Oxford, above the uprising figure which we are accustomed to call Gaia, the Earth, is written the name *Pandora*. In origin there is no doubt that Pandora was simply the Earth-Mother, the All-Giver, but an irresponsible patriarchal mythology changed her into a fair woman dowered with all manner of gifts, the gift of all the gods. Hesiod in the *Works and Days* thus tells the story:

He spake, and they did the will of Zeus, son of Kronos, the Lord;
For straightway the Halting One, the Famous, at his word
Took clay and moulded an image, in form of a maiden fair,
And Athene, the gray-eyed goddess, girt her, and decked her hair.
And about her the Graces divine and our Lady Persuasion set
Bracelets of gold on her flesh; and about her others yet,
The Hours, with their beautiful hair, twined wreaths of blossoms of spring,
While Pallas Athene still ordered her decking in everything.
Then put the Argus-slayer, the marshal of sails, to their place
Tricks and flattering words in her bosom, and thievish ways.
He wrought by the will of Zeus, the Loud-thundering, giving her voice,
Spokesman of gods that he is, and for name of her this was his choice,
PANDORA, because in Olympus the gods joined together then
And *all* of them gave her, a gift, a sorrow to covetous men.[15]

Truly the ways of mythology are not always upwards, the Great Mother has become the Temptress maid.

But the Great Mother was never wholly forgotten. On the Bale Cylix in the British Museum the birth of Pandora or rather her fashioning is depicted. Athena and Hephæstus to either side are busy with her bedecking. But the inscription above her is not Pandora but Anesidora the "sender up of gifts," true epithet of the Earth-Mother. Moreover Pandora's box has become proverbial, but on enquiry it turns out not to be a box at all. The word used by Hesiod is *pithos* and pithos means not a box but a large earthenware jar. These *pithoi* were used by the Greeks as storehouses for grain, wine and oil. Rows of them have come to light at Cnossus, some with remains of grain stored in them. When Pandora opens her box it is not the woman-temptress letting out the woes of mortal man, it is the great Earth-Mother who opens her *pithos*, her store-house of grain and fruits for her children. Through all the glamour of Hesiod's verse, enchanted as he is himself by the vision of the lovely temptress, there gleams also an ugly and malicious theological animus; he is all for the *Father* and the Father will have no great Earth-Goddess in his man-made Olympus. So she who made all things, gods and mortals, is unmade and remade and becomes the plaything of man, his slave, his lure, dowered only with bodily beauty and with a slave's tricks and blandishments. To Zeus, the archpatriarchal bourgeois, the birth of the first woman is a hugh Olympian joke:

He spake and the Sire of men and of gods immortal laughed.

Such a myth rose necessarily and naturally in the social shift from matrilinear to patrilinear conditions.

I. THE GORGON

So far we have seen in the Earth-Mother a figure mild and beneficent, the giver of gifts and the Lady, the Protector of all wild things, but the Earth-Mother had another and a very different aspect. Not only did she bring all things to birth but when live things died she received them back into her bosom. Cicero (*De Natura Deorum*, II. 26. 66) says "all things go back to earth and rise out of the earth"—"dust we are and unto dust do we return." Æschylus (*Choephori*, 127) says:

> Yea, summon Earth, who brings all things to life
> And rears and takes again into her womb.

The Athenians called the dead, "Demeter's people," using the name of their own local Earth-Goddess and at the *Nekusia*, the festival of the dead, they sacrificed to Earth. A ghost is to primitive man a thing of dread, and so the Earth-Mother as Guardian of the dead took on a dread shape, she became a Gorgon. In the British Museum there is a Rhodian plate on which the Mother is figured with a human body and feet and hands in which she grasps two birds, but she is winged and in place of a human head she has a Gorgoneion, a Gorgon-mask.

Such a thing as a Gorgon never of course existed. What then is the Gorgoneion? It is simply a ritual mask, an ugly face made as hideous as possible so as to scare both men and dæmons. Ordinarily the Gorgoneion had pendent tongue, glaring eyes, protruding tusks. It was an image of fear incarnate. Such ritual masks are still in use among savages to scare all evil things, enemies in the flesh and ghostly foes. The Gorgon's head first appears in Greek literature in Homer. Odysseus wishes to hold converse with dead heroes but

> Ere that might be, the ghosts thronged round, in myriads manifold,
> Weird was the magic din they made, a pale green fear gat hold
> Of me, lest for my daring Persephone the dread
> From Hades should send up an awful monster's grizzly head.[16]

Here clearly the Gorgon's head is guardian to the ghosts. We might have thought it would have been more efficacious to send up the Gorgon, the "grizzly monster" itself, but there was no monster to send, only a grizzly head. The dreadful head in all early art representations is prominent, the body is a mere appendage awkwardly tacked on. The Gorgon as monster sprang straight from the Gorgoneion, not the Gorgoneion from the Gorgon. The original ritual mask survives on the ægis of Athena.

But the fertile fancy of the Greeks could not let well or ill alone. New ritual gave them a mask or Gorgon's head; if there was a Gorgon's head there must have been a Gorgon or better still, as things sacred tend to run in Trinities, three Gorgons and so we get (Æschylus, *Prometheus Vinctus*, 798 ff.)

> those sisters three, the Gorgons winged
> With snakes for hair, hated of mortal man,
> None may behold and bear their breathing blight.

But Gorgon slew by the eye, it fascinated, it was in fact a sort of incarnate Evil-Eye. The severed head of course helped out the myth-maker. The severed head, the ritual mask was a fact. Whence came this bodiless, dreadful head? It must needs have been severed from the body of some monster—so a slayer must be provided and Perseus is ready for the part. The remarkable thing is that the Greeks could not in their mythology tolerate the ugliness of the Gorgon. They turned the head of Medusa into the head of a lovely sorrow-stricken woman. In like fashion they could not tolerate the Gorgon form of the Earth-Mother. It was the mission of the Greek artist and the Greek poet to cleanse religion from fear. This is the greatest of debts that we owe to the Greek myth-maker.

II. THE ERINYES-EUMENIDES

This purgation of religion, this casting out or rather transmutation of the spirit of fear is very clearly and beautifully seen in those other Earth-Spirits, the Erinyes. The Erinys is primarily, as the name signifies, the "angry one," the angry ghost—the ghost of the murdered man who calls for vengeance. Æschylus (*Septem*, 988) makes his chorus chant:

> Alas, thou Fate, grievous, dire to be borne,
> And Œdipus! holy Shade,
> Black Erinys, verily, mighty art thou.

The blood of the slain man poisons the earth and the murderer, infecting him like a bacillus breeding disease. So the chorus in the *Choephori* (66) chants:

> Earth that feeds him hath drunk of the gore,
> Blood calling for vengeance flows never more
> But stiffens, and pierces its way
> Through the murderer breeding disease that none may allay.

This is perhaps the most primitive notion of all, the blood itself poisoning the earth, but soon, very soon, the curse of the blood takes personal shape as an embodied curse, haunting, pursuing the murderer.

When Athena in the *Eumenides* (417) asks the Erinyes formally who and what they are, the answer is:

> Curses our name, in haunts below the earth;

and again she demands their rights and prerogatives:

> Man slaying men we drive from out their homes.

Homer who gives to his Olympians such clear outline has no definite shape for these angry Curses of the Underworld, they are terrors unseen. But Æschylus has to give them definite forms because in his *Eumenides* he brings them actually on the stage. How does he figure them? He knows they are Earth-spirits and he makes them half-Gorgons and half-Harpies, only more loathly than either.

The priestess has beheld them in her temple at Delphi and horror-stricken she staggers back to tell what she has seen. They are crouching around Orestes, murderer of his mother:

> Fronting the man I saw a wondrous band
> Of women, sleeping on the seats. But no!
> No women these, but Gorgons—yet methinks
> I may not liken them to Gorgon-shapes.
> Once on a time I saw those pictured things
> That snatch at Phineus' feast, but these, but these
> Are wingless—black, foul utterly. They snore,
> Breathing out noisome breath. From out their eyes
> They ooze a loathly rheum.[17]

Before the time of Æschylus the Erinyes had no fixed form, there was no tradition of art for him to fall back on.

When the mad Orestes sees them (*Choephori*, 1048), he sees only the shapes he knows:

> These are the Gorgon shapes
> "Black robed with tangled tentacles entwined
> Of frequent snakes."

These "frequent snakes" are indeed of the very essence of the Erinys; the snake symbol and incarnation of the dead man is her most primitive form. When Clytæmnestra in the *Eumenides* (126) finds the Erinyes sleeping and would rouse them she cries:

Travail and Sleep, chartered conspirators
Have spent the fell rage of the dragoness.

And in the *Iphigenia in Tauris* (286), the mad Orestes catch-
ing sight of his mother's ghost cries to Pylades:

Dost see her, her the Hades-snake who gapes
To slay me, with dread vipers open-mouthed?

The snake is more than the symbol of the dead, it is the
vehicle of vengeance, the Erinys herself. As such the snake-
symbol proper to the ghost-Erinys is transferred to the living
avenger. Orestes says in the *Choephori* (549):

Myself in serpent's shape
Will slay her.

And when Clytæmnestra pleads for mercy he answers (927):

Nay, for my father's fate hisses thy doom.

Into what are these terrible snake and Gorgon figures, by
the power of the poet's imagination, transformed? They are
transformed into Eumenides, Kindly Ones, and they dwell
henceforth in the cave of the *Semnæ*, the Venerable Ones, on
the Areopagos at Athens. On three votive reliefs found near
Argos the *Semnæ* are figured, and about their forms there is
assuredly nothing frightful, they are not Erinyes, not the
loathly horrors of tragedy, they are staid matronly figures
who carry in their left hands fruit and flowers, tokens of
fertility, and in their right hands snakes, the symbols no
longer of torture and vengeance, but merely symbols of the
underworld as the source of food and wealth. The dedicator
is in each case a woman and on each relief is figured a man

and woman worshipper. The inscription says "a vow to the Eumenides." It may be that husband and wife went to the shrine together and offered the regular sacrifice of honey and water and flowers and a ewe great with young (Æsch., *Eumenides*, 834):

> The first-fruits offered for accomplishment
> Of marriage and for children.

Changed into *Semnæ*, the Erinyes cease from their hideous cries for vengeance and ask Athena what spells they shall henceforth chant over the land. She makes answer:

> Whatever charms wait on fair Victory
> From earth, from dropping dew and from high heaven,
> The wealth of winds that blow to hail the land
> Sunlit, and fruits of earth and teeming flocks
> Untouched of time, safety for human seed.

And the chorus transformed accept henceforth their functions of life and health and growth, and the promised guerdon is chanted in the immortal words:

> No wind to wither trees shall blow
> By our grace it shall be so!
> Nor that, nor shrivelling heat
> On budding plants shall beat
> > With parching dearth
> > To waste their growth,
> Nor any plague of dismal blight come creeping;
> > But teeming, doubled flocks the earth
> > In her season shall bring forth,
> > And ever more a wealthy race
> > Pay reverence for this our grace
> Of spirits that have the rich earth in their keeping.[18]

And as the great procession, purple-robed, torch-bearing, winds up the hill we know that there is "peace upon earth, goodwill to men."

In the case of the Gorgon and the Earth-Mother, and still more with the Erinyes-Eumenides, we see the actual purgation in process, we watch the Greek spirit turn away from fear and anger to peace and love, and the Greek worshipper refuse the ritual of *apotropé*, of repulsion, and choose the free service of *theropeia*, tendance. But in many another mythological figure the process must have gone on unseen. The Olympian gods we have still to study come to us almost wholly purged of all harshness and elements of fear, but here and there, more in ritual than in theology, are indications that the spirit of savagery was close at hand; and always on the breast of Athena, herself incarnation of the Greek spirit though she is, there is the image of the Gorgon, of Fear incarnate.

IV

Demeter and Korè:
The Earth-Mother and
The Earth-Maiden

So long as man lived by hunting he was content to project
the image of the *Lady-of-the-Wild-Things*. But a time came
when he settled down and began to sow seeds and reap grain
and then he must needs image his divinity, express his desire
in a new form that of the Corn-Mother and the Corn-Maiden.
They are but the younger and the older forms, each of the
other. Demeter is not the Earth-Mother, she is goddess of the
fruits of the civilized cultured field of the *tilth*—her name
probably means *spelt*-mother or more generally Grain-
Mother. We may feel surprised that an incarnation of grain-
growing and agriculture should take the form of a woman
but so long as primitive man was taken up with hunting and
fighting, it was natural that woman should be the first agriculturist. There is further a magical reason for this. In his
History of the New World (II. p. 8) Mr. Edward J. Payne
tells us that in America primitive man refused to interfere in
agriculture: he thought it magically dependent for success
on woman and connected with child-bearing. " 'When the
women plant maize' said the Indian to Gumilla, 'the stalk pro-
duces two or three ears; . . . . Why? Because women know
how to produce children. They only know how to plant the
corn so as to ensure its germinating. Then let them plant it;

they know more than we know.'" Just so in the story of
Demeter the functions of Child-Bearer and Seed-Sower are
closely interconnected.

Homer himself as already noted made little account of
Demeter. In the *Iliad* (V. 500), she stands with her yellow
hair at the sacred threshing floor, when men are winnowing—
and "she maketh division of grain and chaff, and the heaps of
chaff grow white." Homer knew Persephone but not as Korè,
not as the daughter of the Corn-Mother, only as the dread
Queen of the Shades below. He knows nothing of the Rape
of Persephone, nor of the world-famed Flower-Gathering.

Homer knew nothing, at least he says nothing of

> that fair field
> Of Enna, where Proserpin gathering flowers,
> Herself a fairer flower, by gloomy Dis
> Was gathered—which cost Ceres all that pain
> To seek her through the world.[19]

It is not Homer who cries:

> O, Proserpina
> For the flowers now, that, frighted, thou letst fall
> From Dis's waggon! [19a]

The modern poet sees deeper. It is as the *daughter* of her
mother Earth that the Queen of the Shades below makes appeal to us, beckons us to her kingdom.

> O daughter of Earth, of my mother, her crown and blossom of
>   birth,
> I am also, I also, thy brother: I go, as I came, unto earth.
> In the night where thine eyes are as moons are in heaven, the
>   night where thou art,
> Where the silence is more than all tunes, and where sleep over-
>   flows from the heart.

Where the poppies are sweet as the rose in our world, and the
    red rose is white,
And the wind falls faint as it blows, with the fume of the flower
    of the night,
And the murmur of spirits that sleep in the shadow of gods from
    afar
Grows dim in thine ears and deep, as the deep dim soul of a star,
In the sweet low light of thy face, under heavens untrod by the
    sun,
Let my soul with their souls find place, and forget what is done
    or undone,
Thou art more than the Gods, who number the days of our tem-
    poral breath,
For these give labour and slumber, but thou, Proserpina, death.[20]

    In all the range of English poetry there is perhaps no fairer
figure than that of Proserpine, and assuredly none more
august.

        Pale, beyond porch and portal,
           Crowned with calm leaves, she stands
        And gathers all things mortal
           With cold immortal hands;
        Her languid lips are sweeter
        Than Love's, who fears to greet her,
        To men that mix and meet her
           From many times and lands.

        She waits for each and other,
           She waits for all men born;
        Forgets the Earth her mother,
           The life of fruits and corn;
        And spring and seed and swallow
        Take wing for her, and follow
        Where summer song rings hollow,
           And flowers are put to scorn.[21]

The two figures of the Mother and the Maid differentiate more and more, and their functions tend to specialize, and on the whole the Mother takes more the physical side, the daughter the spiritual.

If Homer seems to neglect Demeter, ample amends are made by the writer of the Homeric *Hymn* who tells the whole story of the Flower-Gathering and the Rape and the Mourning of the Mother in great detail and in language of singular beauty. The *Hymn*, the manuscript of which is now at Leyden, was found in 1777 in a farmyard at Moscow. Demeter's own sacred pigs had preserved it. It begins almost abruptly with the Flower-Gathering:

Demeter of the beauteous hair, goddess divine, I sing,
Her and the slender-ankled maid, her daughter, whom the King
Aïdoneus seized by Zeus' decree. He found her, as she played
Far from her mother's side, who reaps the corn with golden blade.

The scene was laid in the vale of Enna in Sicily and so Matthew Arnold has it:

O easy access to the hearer's grace
When Dorian shepherds sang to Proserpine!
For she herself had trod Sicilian fields,
She knew the Dorian water's gush divine,
She knew each lily white which Enna yields,
Each Rose with blushing face;
She loved the Dorian pipe, the Dorian train.
But ah, of our poor Thames she never heard!
Her foot the Cumner cowslip never stirred;
    And we should tease her with our plaint in vain! [22]

The poet of the *Hymn* goes on:

She culled the flowers along the mead, she and the daughters fair
Deep-girdled of Okeanos, roses and crocus there;
Pale violets, flags and hyacinths, narcissus set a snare
Of earth by Zeus' decree that he, to whose House all men fare,
Might lure the maid of flower-like face, and have his will of her.

And here the poet pauses to tell of the wonders of the narcissus, a flower in use in the underworld, worn by the *Semnæ*
as their "ancient crown."

The story goes on:

The maid amazed stretched out her hands to take the lovely
    thing,
The wide earth yawned on Nysa's plain and where it yawned,
    the King
Straightway upsprang and caught the maid and sore against her
    will
He, Polydegmon, bore her off in his gold wain, and shrill
Shrieked she and called on father Zeus, most righteous and most
    high,
But no god heard the maiden's voice and no man came nigh.

And then comes the mourning of Demeter. Nine days she
wandered far and wide, seeking her daughter with flaming
torches, till at last she came to Eleusis.

Here follows the long and beautiful episode of the rearing
of the child Demophon by Demeter, disguised as an old serv-
ing woman. The episode was full of meaning to the Greeks,
because the goddess was to them always Kourotrophos, the
child-rearer, but to us who no longer connect seed-sowing
and child-bearing it has lost much of its significance. At last
Demeter casts aside her disguise and in a splendid speech to
the people of Eleusis proclaims her godhead:

I am Demeter, honoured name, a sovran joy and praise
To gods and mortal men. Come ye and bid the folk upraise
A temple great and altar place, below the citadel
High walled, anigh the jutting cliff—, beside the dancers' Well.
Myself will teach my rites and ye, henceforth with pious mind
Shall do them and henceforth my grace to you shall be inclined.
Then as she spake—the goddess cast away her stature old
And changed her shape in wondrous wise, and beauty manifold
She breathed around. From forth her robe a perfumed fragrance
    shed
That makes the heart to yearn. Her golden hair about her head
Streamed and her flesh celestial through the goodly chambers
    glowed—
Like lightning fire from forth the halls, straightway the goddess
    strode.

     .   .   .   .

The women, thro' the livelong night trembling and sore afraid
Tended the boy in vain, and to the glorious goddess prayed.[23]

The goodly temple was builded and the rites established, but the goddess bereft of her daughter still dwelt apart and the earth was barren and desolate. Terrible years of famine did the goddess bring upon mortal, for the earth would not send up her seed and the oxen dragged the crooked ploughs in vain through the furrows. At last Hermes was sent down to Hades to bring back Persephone, but the crafty King gave her to eat of the pomegranate fruit and she that eats of the underworld food must thither return. And so was made the pact of the seasons for a portion of the year; for the winter-time Persephone must abide with her dread husband in the underworld, but for two parts, spring and summer, she should dwell with her mother and the other Immortals:

So they spake. And forthwith did Demeter the garlanded yield
And straightway she let grow the fruits of the loamy field.

And Demeter herself came back to the cornfield:

> Once more the reaper, in the gleam of dawn,
> Will see me by the landmark far away,
> Blessing his field, or seated in the dusk
> Of even, by the lonely threshing-floor,
> Rejoicing in the harvest and the grange.[24]

And the labourer could pray anew:

> O once again may it be mine to plant
> The great fan on her corn heap, while She stands,
> Smiling, with sheaves and poppies in her hands.[25]

The seasons every year come round in their due order; only in Greece did they give birth to human images so lovely.

V

The Maiden-Goddesses as Gift-Givers: Hera, Athena, Aphrodite

Few myths are more familiar than the *Judgment of Paris*.

> Goddesses three to Ida came,
> Immortal strife to settle there—
> Which was the fairest of the three,
> And which the prize of beauty should bear.

The kernel of the myth according to this form of the story is a *kallisteion* or beauty contest. When the gods were assembled at the wedding of Peleus and Thetis, Eris, Strife, threw among them a golden apple. On it was inscribed, "Let the fair one take it," or, as some said, "The apple for the fair one." The three great goddesses Hera, Athena and Aphrodite betake themselves for judgment to the young shepherd Paris, King Priam's son.

The scene is figured on countless ancient vases but on one and one only is it figured as a Judgment. The design in question is from a late red-figured crater in the Bibliothèque Nationale in Paris. The goddesses are grouped round the young Phrygian shepherd and in characteristic fashion they are preparing for a beauty contest, while Hermes, who has brought them, tells to Paris his mission. Hera is gazing well satisfied in a mirror and sets her veil in order; Aphrodite stretches out her fair arm that a love-god may fasten a "bracelet of gold on her flesh"; and Athena, watched only by a large serious faithful dog, goes to a little fountain shrine and, clean goddess as she is, tucks her gown about her and has a good wash.

And in our hearts we cry with Œnone:

> "O Paris,
> Give it to Pallas!" but he heard me not,
> Or hearing would not hear me, woe is me! [26]

In every other representation of the scene not only is the apple absent as even here but the scene depicted is not a beauty-contest at all but a choice of gifts offered to Paris. Each of the three goddesses indifferently holds flowers or fruit, but these are simply decorations, attributes. The three goddesses are gift-givers, grace-givers and they each offer in turn their characteristic gifts to Paris; it is for him to choose and on his choice depends the issue of the Trojan war. But before Paris was there, the eternal motive of the Choice was there, the Choice that comes more or less to each and every man. The exact elements of the "Choice" vary; Athena is sometimes Wisdom, sometimes War, Hera is grandeur or royalty, Aphrodite always love and Beauty. The late Alexandrian and Roman story is by the right understanding of it redeemed from the vulgarity inherent in a beauty contest and complicated by the further vulgarity of a bribe. But more than that; we begin to understand what each and all of these Maiden-Goddesses are, they are Charites, Grace-Bringers, Gift-Givers, and they themselves,—all forms of the Earth-Mother are only distinguishable by their gifts,—they are in fact their own gifts and graces incarnate.

It is not only in the so-called "Judgment of Paris" that the three goddesses appear as gift-givers. We find them dowering mortals in the *Odyssey*, the daughters of Pandareus, but not this time as rivals. A fourth, Artemis, is their helper.

Homer puts the story into the mouth of Penelope, who tells of Pandareus' daughters:

Their father and their mother dear died by the gods' high doom,
The maidens were left orphans, alone within their home;
Fair Aphrodite gave them curds and honey of the bee
And lovely wine, and Hera made them very fair to see,
And wise beyond all women-folk. And holy Artemis
Made them to wax in stature, and Athene for their bliss
Taught them all glorious handiworks of woman's artifice.[27]

The gifts are here distributed rather differently. Hera, not Athena, gave wisdom and Aphrodite gives only honey and curds to these maidens too young for love, but it may be that the figures of the Gift-Givers had not as yet completely crystallized. We will take them in order.

I. HERA

It may seem strange to find Hera among the Maidens: she is to us all wife and Queen; in fact by her marriage with Zeus she becomes the typical Bride and their Holy Marriage is at once the prototype and the consecration of all human wedlock. But the name *Hera* means *Year* and there is not wanting evidence that she was at first the Year, the fruits of the Year incarnate. In far away Arcadia, where things still went on in primitive fashion, Hera, at Stymphalus, had three surnames and three corresponding sanctuaries. She was called and worshipped as Child, when married she was called *Teleia*, the Full-Grown, and last she had her sanctuary as *Chera*, Widow. The symbolism of the three surnames is transparent. In the Spring season, she is Child or Maiden, in Summer and Autumn she is Full-Grown, and in Winter she is a Widow. Her desolation is like the mourning of Demeter. Hera, then, as Year-Goddess, stood for the three seasons, figured as the three stages of a woman's life. At her Sacred Marriage, Homer (*Il.*, XIV. 347 ff.) tells us: "beneath them the divine earth sent forth fresh new grass and dewy lotus and crocus and hyacinth thick and soft, that raised them aloft from the ground. Therein they lay and were clad on with a fair golden cloud whence fell drops of glittering dew." It is the very image of the fertility of early summer.

But there was another side. Signs are not lacking that this marriage of Hera with Zeus was a forced alliance and certainly not from the beginning. Long before her connection with Zeus she had, as a great matrilinear goddess like the Earth-Mother, reflected the seasons of the year and the stages of woman's life. In the old Argonautic legend Hera is Queen in her own right of Thessaly and patron, in the old matriarchal fashion, of the hero Jason. She, the old Pelasgian Queen, is the really dominant power. The marriage of Zeus and Hera is in fact a forcible one and it reflects the subjugation of the indigenous people by incoming Northerners. Only thus can we account for the fact that the divine husband and wife are in constant unseemly conflict. Of course a human motive is alleged; Hera is jealous, Zeus in constant exasperation. But the real reason is a racial conflict. The worshippers of Zeus and Hera, Achæans and Argives, were after long conflict barely reconciled. In actual cult, Hera reigned alone in the great Argive Heræum, alone also at Samos; her temple even at Olympia is far older and quite distinct from that of Zeus. In Homer she is represented as the jealous and quarrelsome wife; really, she is the image, the projection of the turbulent nation, a princess coërced, but never really subdued by an alien conqueror. The real, shadow wife is Dione, abandoned by Zeus at

Dodona when he entered Greece. It is perhaps for this reason that Ox-eyed Hera fails to make lasting appeal to either art or literature.

It is quite other with Athena. As Professor Gilbert Murray has well said: "*Athena is an ideal and a mystery: the ideal of wisdom, of incessant labour, of almost terrifying purity, seen through the light of some mystic and spiritual devotion like, but transcending the love of man for woman.*" If the claim of Hera to be Maiden be doubtful, there is no question in Athena's case; she is *the* Parthenos, the Maiden, her temple the Parthenon. Natural motherhood she renounced, but she is foster-mother of heroes, and their constant guardian and guide; such is her relationship to Theseus, to Perseus, to Heracles and to Erichthonius.

It should be noted at the outset that her name in its full form, *Athenaia*, is adjectival; she is *She of Athens*, the Athenian maid, "Pallas, our Lady of Athens." Plato in the *Laws* (796) clearly expresses this. He is speaking of the armed Athena and says: "methinks our *Korè* and Mistress who dwells among us, joying her in the sport of dancing, was not minded to play with empty hands, but adorned her with her panoply and thus accomplished her dance, and it is fitting that in this our youths and maidens should imitate." Plato's psychology was that of his own day; naturally he inverts the order of procedure. It was Athena who "imitated" her maidens and youths, she who was the incarnation of their every thought and action, dancing in armour as they danced, fighting as they fought. To write the story of the making of Athena is to trace the spiritual history of the city of Athens.

Athena, at the outset, like Mother-Earth from whom she sprang, was closely linked with the life of plants and animals.

Her attendant bird was the owl which still, if we climb the Acropolis at moonlight, may be heard and seen hooting among the ruins. The image of the owl was stamped on Athenian coins. Athena's "owls" were current far and wide. Still more intimately associated with her was the snake, again a survival from her aspect as Earth-Goddess. The "house-guarding" snake was, it may be conjectured, the earliest form of every local Korè. At Athens the snake was the fate, the guardian genius of the city before that genius took on human form. Herodotus (VIII. 41. 3) tells us how when the Persians besieged the city, the guardian snake left untasted its honey-cake, the sacrificial food offered to it month by month, and when the priestess told the people of the portent, the Athenians the more readily and eagerly forsook their city, inasmuch as *it seemed* that the goddess had abandoned their citadel. On a late red-figured lecythus in the Central Museum at Athens is a representation of the Judgment or rather Choice of Paris. Only one goddess is present, Athena. By her side stands a great snake, equal to the goddess in height and majesty. The vase-painter seems dimly aware that goddess and divine snake are one. In the masterpiece of Phidias, the great chryselephantine statue of Athena, beneath her shield still crouched the guardian snake.

Yet more sacred and intimate is her association with the olive:

> The holy bloom of the olive, whose hoar leaf
> High in the shadowy shrine of Pandrosus
> Hath honor of us all,

as Swinburne has it in his *Erechtheus*.

Long ago the Chorus in the *Œdipus at Colonus* of Sophocles chanted the glory of the olive tree of Athens:

And this country for her own has what no Asian land hath known,

Nor ever yet in the great Dorian Pelops island has it grown,
The untended, the self-planted, self-defended from the foe,
Sea-gray, children-nurturing olive tree that here delights to grow.
None may take, nor touch, nor harm it, headstrong youth nor
      age grown bold,
For the Round of Morian Zeus has been its watcher from of old;
He beholds it and Athena, thine own sea-gray eyes behold.[28]

Pausanias (I. 27. 2) says that the olive tree was produced
by the goddess at the time of her contest for the land, as a
token of her power, but, he adds, there is also a story that the
tree was burnt to the ground when the Persians set fire to the
city of the Athenians and that after it had been burnt down,
it sprang up and grew as much as two cubits in a day. The
olive tree it is clear was the fate, the *Moira*, of the city, intimately bound up with its life.

Poseidon and Athena fought for the city of Athens:

> A noise is arisen against her of waters
> A sound as of battle came up from the sea.

Strife, bitter strife

> Twixt god and god had risen which heavenlier name
> Should here stand hallowed, whose more liberal grace
> Should win this city's worship, and own land
> To which of these do reverence.

Poseidon with his trident smote the Acropolis rock and forth
there sprang a well of strange bright brine; he brought forth
the horse, but Athena set for her sign the olive tree.

The high gods met in judgment and they

> Gave great Pallas the strife's fair stake,
> The Lordship and care of the lovely land,

> The grace of the town that hath on it for crown
>   But a headband to wear
>   Of violets one-hued with her hair,
> For the vales and the green, high places of earth
>   Hold nothing so fair,
> And the depths of the sea know no such birth
>   Of the manifold births they bear.

In terms of pre-history, what the famous strife means is this: Athena was the Maiden of the oldest stratum of population, before the incoming of the Minoans. Poseidon stands always for the Minoan aristocracy, wealthy, haughty. The rising democracy revived the ancient maiden figure, but transmuted her whole being and made her an incarnation of the new, free, democratic city.

> Dear city of men without master or lord,
> Fair fortress and fostress of sons born free,
> Who stand in her sight and in thine, O Sun,
> Slaves of no man, subjects of none;
> A wonder enthroned on the hills and the sea,
> A maiden crowned with a fourfold glory,
> That none from the pride of her head may rend.
> Violet and olive leaf, purple and hoary,
> Song wreath and story, the fairest of fame,
>   Flowers that the winter can blast not or bend;
>   A light upon earth as the sun's own flame,
>   A name as his name,
> Athens, a praise without end.[29]

The real object of adoration to the Athenian was not a goddess but the city herself, "immortal mistress of a band of lovers," and in the passion of this adoration they would lift her from all earthly contact, they would not have her born as other mortals.

Her life, as the lightning, was flashed from the light of her
    Father's head.

It is this that lends to the figure of Athena an aloofness, that
makes of her, for all her beauty, something of an abstraction,
an unreality; she is Reason, Light and Liberty, a city

> Based on a crystalline sea
> Of thought and its eternity.

III. APHRODITE AND EROS

    Perhaps in contemplating the figure of Athena we have
been conscious of a certain strain, a certain contradiction, and
that after all, as Althæa says,

> A woman, armed, makes war upon herself,
> Unwomanlike, and treads down use and wont
> And the sweet common honour that she hath,
> Love, and the cry of children, and the hand
> Trothplight and mutual mouth of marriages.[30]

If so, we turn with relief to the figure of Aphrodite which
has not only a singular loveliness but a singular simplicity and
unity.

We have seen thee, O Love, thou art fair: thou art goodly,
    O Love,
Thy wings make light in the air, as the wings of a dove,
Thy feet are as winds that divide the stream of the sea;
Earth is thy covering to hide thee, the garment of thee.

    Aphrodite is, perhaps, the fairest of all the forms of the
Earth-Mother; like her, she has a sacred bird, the dove, and

like her she has a son, the attribute of Motherhood, Eros. Let the Mother come first.

Aphrodite is maiden in her perennial radiance, but virgin she is not. Rather she is the eternal *Nymphe*, the Bride, but the bride of the old matrilinear order, intolerant of patriarchal monogamy. Once admitted to Olympus, a regulation husband had to be found for her, the craftsman Hephæstus, but the link is plainly artificial. Always in Olympus she is something of an alien, perhaps because it was realized that she came from Cyprus. Homer (*Od.*, VIII. 361 ff.), when Ares and Aphrodite escape from the snare set them, says:

> Straightway forth sprang the twain;
> To savage Thrace went Ares, but Cypris with sweet smile
> Hied her to her fair altar place in pleasant Paphos isle.

Ares and Aphrodite have no link in ritual, but are the two counter-powers of Strife and Harmony; philosophy made of them metaphorical use. It is to a Roman poet and a Roman philosopher, using Greek material, that we owe the august image of Venus Genetrix, mistress of Mars, the War-God; and to their marriage (to his mind) was due the *Pax Romana*.

> Of Rome, the Mother, of men and gods the pleasure,
> Fostering Venus, under heaven's gliding signs
> Thou the ship-bearing sea, fruit-bearing land
> Still hauntest, since by thee each living thing
> Takes life and birth and sees the light of the Sun.
>
> Thee goddess, the winds fly from, thee the clouds
> And thine approach, for thee the dædal earth
> Sends up sweet flowers, the ocean levels smile
> And heaven shines with floods of light appeased.
>
> Thou, since alone thou rulest all the world,

Nor without thee can any living thing
Win to the shores of light and love and joy,
Goddess, bid thou throughout the seas and land
The works of furious Mars quieted cease.[31]

Touched though the words are with a stiff majesty that is all Roman, yet the thought is wholly Greek. Just such a figure is Aphrodite, in the *Homeric Hymn*, when "she came to many-fountained Ida, she, the mother of wild beasts, and made straight for the steading in the mountain, while behind her came fawning the beasts, grey wolves and lions, fiery-eyed, and bears and swift pards, insatiate pursuers of the roe-deer. Glad was she at the sight of them and sent desire into their breasts." She is the mother of all life throughout the world, a veritable "Lady of the Wild Things."

She was goddess of life upon the earth, but especially goddess of the sea, as became her island birth:

For the West Wind breathed to Cyprus and lifted her tenderly
And bore her down the billow and the stream of the sounding
sea
In a cup of delicate foam. And the Hours in wreaths of gold
Uprose in joy as she came, and laid on her, fold on fold,
Fragrant raiment immortal, and a crown on her deathless head.[32]

She is of the upper air as well as of the sea, and on a cylix with white ground, in the British Museum, the vase-painting in a design of marvellous beauty and delicacy has set her to sail through heaven on a great swan. Aphrodite is, I think, the only goddess who in passing to the upper air did not lose something of her humanity and reality. It may be that as knowledge and command over things natural advanced, the mystery and godhead of nature was more and more lost in science. But the mystery of life and of love, that begets life, remains unsolved and the godhead of Aphrodite remains.

Perhaps the loveliest and certainly the most significant of the images of Aphrodite in ancient art is on a red-figured cylix in the Berlin Museum (Fig. 5), signed by the master Hieron. It is part of a representation of the "Choice" of Paris. Aphrodite stands erect in flowing drapery and veiled, under her left arm is her dove. All around her head play her children, the Erôtes. And what are the Erôtes? Who and what is Erôs? He is a Life-Spirit, as unlike as possible to the fat, idle Cupid of the Romans. When a man dies, his spirit, his life-force escapes from his mouth in the guise of a small winged figure, a *Ker*, as the Greeks called it; just such a *Ker*, only of Life, is Erôs. He is no idle, impish urchin, still less is he the romantic passion between man and woman, he is just the spirit of life, a thing to man with his moral complexity sometimes fateful and even terrible, but to young things in spring, to live plants and animals a thing glad and kind. So the vase-painter figured love,—a wingèd sprite, carrying a flowering branch over land and sea. So Theognis wrote:

Love comes at his hour, comes with the flowers of spring,
    Leaving the land of his birth,
Kypros, beautiful isle. Love comes, scattering
    Seed for man upon earth.[33]

The winged Erôtes hover about Aphrodite, carrying flower sprays and wreaths, bringing gifts to the Gift-Giver, they too being Spirits of Grace and Life.

Erôs is everywhere, he moves upon the face of the waters, he hides in a maiden's cheek. The Chorus in the *Antigone* sing:

O Thou of War unconquered, thou Erôs,
    Spoiler of garnered gold, who liest hid
    In a girl's cheek, under the dreaming lid,
While the long night-time flows,

> O rover of the seas, O terrible one,
>   In wastes and wild wood-caves
>   None may escape thee, none:
>   Not of the heavenly Gods, who live alway,
>   Not of bad men, who vanish ere the day:
>   And he who finds thee, raves.[34]

It is worth noting that as the Earth-Mother developed into a
Trinity of Grace-Givers, so Erôs develops a triple form. On
a red-figured *stamnus* in the British Museum, we have three
beautiful love-gods, figured flying over the sea; they are
Erôs, Himeros (Longing) and Pothos (Regret); they carry,
one, a hare, the love-gift of the Greeks, one, a flowering
branch, one, a *tænia* or ribbon-like scarf. On the reverse of
the vase are figured the three Sirens and possibly the three
Sirens suggested the three Erôtes. But the triple form took
no permanent hold on either art or literature.

To some extent at Athens, owing to the poignant character
of attachments between man and man, Aphrodite suffered
eclipse and Erôs her son became dominant. Alcman's words
seem to be for a time realized:

> There is no Aphrodite. Hungry Love
> Plays, boy-like, with light feet upon the flowers.

The art-type of Erôs, as *ephebus,* is perfected about this time.
Still even in the fifth century B.C., the noblest hymns to Erôs
were inspired by the love of man for woman.

Such is the hymn, chanted by the Chorus in the *Hippolytus*
of Euripides:

> Erôs, Erôs, who blindest, tear by tear,
>   Men's eyes with hunger; thou swift Foe, that pliest
> Deep in our hearts joy like an edgèd spear;
> Come not to me with Evil, haunting near,

FIGURE 5 *Aphrodite and Erôtes*

Wrath on the wind, nor jarring of the clear
  Wings' music as thou fliest!
There is no shaft that burneth, not in fire,
Not in wild stars, far off and flinging fear,
As in thine hands the shaft of All Desire,
  Erôs, Child of the Highest!

We have travelled far from the gentle Life-Spirits carrying flowers.

Another choric hymn in the *Hippolytus* seems equally addressed to Mother and Son:

Thou comest to bend the pride
  Of the hearts of God and man,
Cypris; and by thy side,
  In earth-encircling span,
He of the changing plumes,
The Wing that the world illumes,
As over the leagues of land flies he,
Over the salt and sounding sea.

For mad is the heart of Love,
  And gold the gleam of his wing;
And all to the spell thereof
  Bend, when he makes his spring;
All life that is wild and young
  In mountain and wave and stream,
All that of earth is sprung,
  Or breathes in the red sunbeam;
Yea, and Mankind. O'er all a royal throne,
Cyprian, Cyprian, is thine alone! [35]

And with the figure of Aphrodite comes back the ancient glory of the Earth-Mother.

VI

Artemis

The figure of Artemis is in a sense more primitive than that
of either Athena or Aphrodite. She is nearer akin to the "Lady
of the Wild Things." Her local cults are not without traces
of primitive savagery. Pausanias (VII. 18. 12) tells us of a
yearly holocaust offered to Artemis at Patræ, which exactly
resembled that of the Great-Mother at Hierapolis. After de-
scribing the altar surrounded by a circle of green logs of
wood and approached by an inclined plane made of earth, he
tells of the procession of the virgin priestess in a car drawn
by deer. Of the sacrifice itself he says it was not merely a
state affair but popular among private people. "For they bring
and cast upon the altar living things of all sorts both edible
birds and all manner of victims, also wild boars and deer and
fawns and some even bring the cubs of wolves and bears, and
others full grown beasts. I saw indeed a bear and other beasts
struggling to get out of the first force of the flames and escap-
ing by sheer strength. But those who threw them in drag
them up again on to the fire, I never heard of any one being
wounded by the wild beasts." Even in the civilized days of
Pausanias the service of the Huntress-Maid was horrible and

bloodthirsty. It is well perhaps for once to realize from what imminent savagery the Olympian divinities had emerged.

Compare with this the ritual of the Great-Mother at Hierapolis, as observed by Pausanias (IV. 32. 6). In the court of the sanctuary were kept all manner of beasts and birds. "Consecrated oxen, horses, eagles, bears and lions who never hurt any one but are holy and tame to handle." But these tame holy beasts were kept for a horrid purpose! Lucian (*De Syr. Dea*, 49) thus describes the holocaust: "Of all the festivals, the greatest that I know of they hold at the beginning of the spring. Some call it the *Pyre*, and some the Torch. At this festival they do as follows. They cut down great trees and set them up in the courtyard. Then they bring sheep and goats and other live beasts and hang them up on the trees. They also bring birds and clothes and vessels of gold and silver. When they have made all ready, they carry the victims round the trees and set fire to them and straightway they are all burned." And again at Messene, Pausanias (IV. 31. 7) saw the same horrid ritual. He tells us of "a hall of the Curetes, where they sacrifice without distinction all animals, beginning with oxen and goats and ending with birds; they throw them all into the fire." And who are the Curetes? Who but the young men, the ministrants of the Great-Mother.

The sacrifice at Messene to Laphria is scarcely less horrible than that of Tauris, where the local goddess demanded human blood. Against this the later conscience of Greece revolted. Euripides (*Iphigenia in Tauris*) makes Iphigenia, doomed to sacrifice her brother, cry out against Artemis:

> Herself doth drink this blood of slaughtered men?
> Could ever Leto, she of the great King
> Beloved, be mother to so gross a thing?
> These tales be false, false as those feastlings wild
> Of Tantalus and Gods that love a child.

> This land of murderers to its god hath given
> Its own lust: evil dwelleth not in heaven.

Again the Leader of the chorus protests that human sacrifice is no Greek offering and thus adjures the goddess:

> O holy one, if it afford
> 　　Thee joy, what these men bring to thee,
> Take thou their sacrifice, which we
> 　　By law of Hellas, hold abhorred.

Artemis herself, the story went, had substituted in her sacrifice a fawn for the maiden Iphigenia. Iphigenia cries:

> Tell him that Artemis my soul did save,
> I wot not how, and to the altar gave
> A fawn instead: the which my father slew,
> Not seeing, deeming that the sword he drew
> Struck me. But she had borne me far away
> And left me in this land.[36]

These substitution stories,—the fawn for Iphigenia, the ram for Isaac,—all mark the transition from human to animal sacrifice.

The next rite, though very primitive, shows Artemis in gentler guise. On the Acropolis at Athens was a precinct of Artemis Brauronia and in it an image made by Praxiteles. Within this precinct went on the *arkteia* or "bear-service." In the *Lysistrata* of Aristophanes (641) the chorus of women sing of the benefits they have received from the state and how they were reared at its expense. "As soon as I was seven years old I became an *Errephorus*, then when I was ten, I was grinder to our Sovereign Lady, then, wearing the saffron robe, *I was a bear* in the Brauronian festival." In Arcadia it does not surprise us to find that Artemis herself, bearing the euphemistic title of *Calliste*, "the fairest," was a bear, nor that one of her faithless worshippers was turned into a bear. Among the rude dwellers in Arcadia a bear may well have been a creature greatly to be dreaded and most eagerly to be propitiated. But in the Christian era to find in civilized Athens on her sacred hill a bear cult is a striking instance of the tenacity of ancient tradition. The precinct must have been a strange sight; the little girls of Athens wrapped in yellow bear skins would dance or crouch bear fashion before the goddess. A goat was sacrificed to Artemis and till the next festival the little girls were safe from marriage. They had accomplished their bear-service. After a while it would seem they got shy of the rude ritual, since, by the time of Aristophanes, for the bear skin was substituted a saffron robe and henceforth we hear more of the dedication of raiment than the dancing of bears. But always these well-born, well-bred little Athenian girls who danced as bears to Artemis must to the end of their days have thought reverently of the might of the Great-She-Bear. Among the Apaches to-day we are told "only ill-bred Americans, or Europeans who have never had any 'raising' would think of speaking of the Bear, or indeed even of the Snake without employing the reverential prefix 'Ostin,' meaning Old One, the equivalent of the Roman 'Senator.' "

The first time I visited Athens I was turning over the fragments in the Acropolis Museum, then little more than a lumber room. In a rubbish pile in the corner of the room I had the great happiness to light on the small stone figure of a bear. One furry paw was sticking out and caught my eye. Some maiden richer or more pious than the rest had offered to the goddess this image of herself, a small bear comfortably seated on its hind legs. Precisely where the bear was discovered I failed to find out, but originally she must have been set up in the Brauronian precinct.

It seems probable that from the holocaust service arose the

figure of the Huntress Artemis; she, in whose honour the wild
and tame beasts were slain, became herself the slayer. In
Homer uniformly Artemis is the Huntress. When the Caly-
donians (*Il.*, IX. 533) fail to bring their Hecatomb, it is the
Archer-Goddess who "was wroth and sent against them a
creature of heaven, a fierce wild boar, white-tusked, that
wrought sore ill continually on Oineus' garden land," and it
is the Maiden-Huntress of Calydon that the chorus in the
Atalanta hail:

> Come with bows bent and with emptying of quivers,
>   Maiden most perfect, lady of light,
> With a noise of winds and many rivers,
>   With a clamour of waters and with might;
> Bind on thy sandals, O thou most fleet,
> Over the splendour and speed of thy feet;
> For the faint east quickens, the wan west shivers,
>   Round the feet of the day and the feet of the night.[37]

It may surprise us perhaps that a woman goddess is chosen
by the Greeks to be huntsman-in-chief. Assuredly the clois-
tered Greek woman did not, modern fashion, join the chase.
But the difficulty disappears, if we remember that the aspect
of huntress was taken over from the "Lady of the Wild
Things" and probably by way of the holocaust.

Artemis is not only Slayer of the wild beasts. She shares
with Apollo the ministry of death to mortals. In the *Odyssey*
Homer tells of the fair island of Syria, a good land,

>   with oxen and with sheep
> Well stored, and laden vines and cornfields deep,
> And hunger never comes upon the folk,
> Nor sore diseases that make mortals weep.
> But to the tribes of men, when old they grow

> Therein, the Archer of the silver bow,
> Apollo, comes with Artemis, and thus
> With shafts that hurt not strikes and lays them low.[38]

Artemis may have her aspect as death-dealer to women merely as the correlative of Apollo; on the other hand it is perhaps more likely that she here reflects the darker underworld side of the Earth-Mother.

One aspect of Artemis is undoubtedly that of the Moon. It should be observed that as soon as the Greeks or any other people come to realize that the seasons are controlled by the moon and sun, and that their food supply is therefore influenced by these potencies, they tend to let their earth divinities take on certain attributes of sun and moon. The worship of the moon naturally precedes that of the sun, because the appearances and disappearances of the moon, being at shorter intervals, naturally first arrested attention. The old error of Naturism was to suppose that sun or moon exhausted the whole content of a god or goddess. The new psychology points out that into the content of man's experiences and hence into his expression of that experience in the figures of his divinities, there enter at a certain stage of civilization elements drawn not only from the earth but from the heavenly bodies, from sun and moon, and first it would seem from moon. The moon is an arresting object, a thing of spectral terror, staring with dull, pitiless eye.

> Setebos, Setebos, and Setebos!
> Thinketh, He dwelleth i' the cold o' the moon.[39]

Phœbus is still for us the Sun:

> Hark, hark, the lark at heaven's gate sings
> And Phoebus 'gins arise.

And who is *Phœbe*, Artemis, but the Moon with silver bow? So Swinburne's huntsman addresses her, in the *Atalanta in Calydon*:

> Maiden, and mistress of the months and stars
> Now folded in the flowerless fields of heaven,

and again the chorus:

> When the hounds of spring are on winter's traces,
> The mother of months in meadow or plain
> Fills the shadows and windy places
> With lisp of leaves and ripple of rain.

The moon has her dark and spectral side, but this is taken over by Hecate, leaving the brightness for Artemis. Hecate is compact of magic and spells. In the second *Idyll* of Theocritus we have the picture of Simætha, the magician,—Simætha who in the anguish of her slighted love invokes Hecate, who is also Artemis, and seeks to lure her lover back by incantations with the magic wheel on which is bound the lynx, the wry-neck. The scene is fitly laid in the moonlight. Simætha sings:

> Lo! now the barley smoulders in the flame,
>   Thestylis, wretch! thy wits are woolgathering!
> Am I a laughing stock, to thee a Shame?
>   Scatter the grain, I say, the while I sing;
>   "The bones of Delphis I am scattering;
> Bird, magic Bird bring the man back to me."

> Next do I burn this wax, God helping me,
> So may the heart of Delphis melted be,
>   This brazen wheel I whirl, so as before

Restless may he be whirled about my door.
"Bird, magic Bird bring the man home to me."
Next will I burn these husks. O Artemis
  Hast power hell's adamant to shatter down
And every stubborn thing. Hark! Thestylis,
  Hecate's hounds are baying up the town,
  The Goddess at the crossways. Clash the gong.

.   .   .   .

Lo now the sea is still. The winds are still.
The ache within my heart is never still.[40]

In the *Hippolytus* of Euripides, Artemis is all huntress-maiden and as such she is sworn foe to Aphrodite. It is Aphrodite who speaks the prologue and the whole speech is charged with the never dying hatred of the voluptuary for the ascetic:

Great among men, and not unnamed am I,
The Cyprian, in God's inmost halls on high,
And wheresoe'er from Pontus to the far
Red West men dwell, and see the glad day-star,
And worship Me, the pious heart I bless,
And wreck that life that lives in stubbornness.

And then she tells how Hippolytus, reared in strait ways, scorns her and

hath dared, alone of all Trozên,
To hold me least of spirits and most mean,
And spurns my spell and seeks no woman's kiss.
But great Apollo's sister, Artemis,
He holds of all most high, gives love and praise,
And through the wild dark woods for ever strays,
He and the Maid together, with swift hounds
To slay all angry beasts from out these bounds.

And as the goddess leaves the stage, enter Hippolytus with his huntsmen and Hippolytus sings:

> Follow, O follow me,
>   Singing on your ways
> Her in whose hand are we,
> Her whose own flock we be,
> The Zeus-Child, the Heavenly;
>   To Artemis be praise!

And the huntsmen make answer:

> Hail to thee, Maiden blest,
> Proudest and holiest:
> God's Daughter, great in bliss,
> Leto-born, Artemis!
> Hail to thee, Maiden, far
> Fairest of all that are,
>   Yea, and most high thine home,
> Child of the Father's Hall;
> Hear, O most virginal,
> Hear, O most fair of all,
>   In high God's golden dome.[41]

Artemis in the *Hippolytus* is austere to the point of in-humanity. But her maidenhood can take on a gentler and more homely aspect. An epigram from the *Anthology* shows, clearly and simply, how in the worship the maidenhood of the worshipper was mirrored:

> Maid of the Mere, Timaretè here brings,
>   Before she weds, her cymbals, her dear ball
> To Thee, a Maid, her maiden offerings,
>   Her snood, her maiden dolls, their clothes and all.

Hold, Leto's child, above Timaretè
Thine hand and keep her virginal like thee.[42]

Note the "before she weds." It was no perpetual virginity that
she vowed.

There is a passage in the *Hippolytus* which points to an
aspect of Artemis quite other than that of the Virgin-Huntress
and it is of the first importance for the full understanding of
her nature.

When the huntsmen have ended their chant, Hippolytus
himself advances to the shrine of Artemis, with a wreath in
his hand. Arrian in his *Treatise on Hunting* (33) tells us that
hunters must pay homage to Artemis *Agrotera*, She-of-the-
Wild, must pour libation, crown her, sing hymns and offer
first-fruits of the game taken, and must also crown their dogs,
and that dogs and masters must feast together. Hippolytus
does not stay to crown his dogs, but straightway invokes the
goddess thus:

> Mine own, my one desire,
>   Virgin most fair
> Of all the virgin choir,
> Hail, O most pure, most perfect, loveliest one,
>   Lo! in my hand I bear,
> Woven for the circling of thy long, gold hair,
>   Culled leaves and flowers from places which the sun
>   In spring long shines upon.
> Where never shepherd hath driven flock to graze,
>   Nor any grass is mown;
> But there sound, thro' all the sunny sweet warm days,
>   Mid the green holy place,
>   The wild bees' wing alone.
> And maiden reverence tends the fair things there,
> And watereth all of them with sprinkled showers,
>   Whoso is chaste of spirit utterly

May gather there the leaves and fruit and flowers,—
    The unchaste never.
But thou, O goddess, and dearest love of mine,
    Take and about thine hair
    This anadem entwine
    Take and for my sake wear.[43]

Great stress is laid of course on the purity and sanctity of the garland and the place whence it was culled. It is clear, I think, that the place was a "garden enclosed" and the gardens of the ancients were not so much gardens for flowers and fruits, as enclosures for the growing of medicinal herbs. Medea had such a garden full of laurel and asphodel and mandragora and all-heal and the like. Sophocles wrote a play, which is lost to us, called the *Root-Cutters,* and in it he described Medea cutting her evil herbs by moonlight. Such herbs were good for medicine or for magic; the two in those days were not far asunder. Dr. Rendel Harris, in his fascinating *Ascent of Olympus,* has drawn attention to the importance of these herbal gardens in ancient religion and he tells us the very herb to which Artemis owes her name, the *artemisia,* a wormwood sometimes called mugwort. Garlands were made on St. John's Eve of this and other magic herbs, and they possessed the power of "dispelling dæmons." On a manuscript of the eleventh century Artemis is figured presenting the mugwort to Chiron, the Centaur. The herb Artemisia grew abundantly on Mt. Taygetus, the favourite haunt of Artemis. Two strands it would seem have gone to the making of the Goddess, the Earth-Mother from the South and the Maid-Magician, the Healer of the North.

VII

⌕⌕

Apollo

No God is more Greek or perhaps so Greek as Apollo. He
stands indeed as the incarnation and utterance of the Greek
way of thinking. When, in the *Ode to the Nativity*, Milton
would mark the eclipse and overthrow by Christianity of the
Greek Pantheon he need only say:

> Apollo from his shrine
> Can no more divine,
> With hollow shriek the steep of Delphos leaving.

Moreover in Olympus itself he seems to occupy a position
second only to Zeus himself. At his coming the Homeric
Hymn tells us: "as he fares thro' the house of Zeus, the Gods
tremble, yea, and rise up all from their thrones, as he draws
near with his shining bended bow." Only Leto his mother
remains seated. His first Epiphany in the *Iliad* (I. 43 ff.) is as
death-dealer. Phœbus Apollo came down from the height of
Olympus, wroth in his heart, his bow and quiver on his
shoulders, and his arrows clanged as the god moved in his
wrath, and he walked like unto the night. He is sudden, irre-
sistible. For nine days he let fly his arrows through the host
and men and mules and fleet dogs perished of the pestilence.

Apollo in the *Iliad* is not prophet, not musician. He is the Far-Darter, the death-dealer, "most deadly of all the gods."

But if he brings disease and death, he also brings healing. Apollo, like Artemis, is at least in part a Northerner and like Artemis a Healer. In a remarkable article,[44] Professor Grace Macurdy has shown beyond the possibility of doubt whence Apollo came and what, in one of his aspects, he originally was. No title of Apollo is more frequent and more reverent than that of *Pæon*. Pæon is god of Pæonia and Pæonia is the land of the styptic peony. In the *Iliad* (V. 899 ff.) Zeus chides Ares for whining about his wound but promises he shall be healed. "Thus spake he and bade Pæon heal, and Pæon, putting the pain-allaying herbs on Ares' wound, healed him for Ares was immortal. Like as when fig-juice by its quick action curdles the white milk which is liquid, but curdles quickly at the stirring, so Pæon healed fierce Ares." The peony was the first styptic to be discovered, it was brought to Greece through Persia from China and Japan where it is still held in high honour as a magic herb of portentous might. The ancient herbalists teem with its praises. The red single species still grows on the Balkans; of old it grew there in "Apollo's ancient garden." Apollo and Artemis were both herbalists and it may be that from their common function, the notion of their twin-ship arose.

Apollo was worshipped by the Hyperboreans. And who are they? Not, I think, as the name used to be explained, the people beyond Boreas the North-Wind,—but, following again Professor Macurdy, the people beyond Bora; Bora (like its Slavonic correlative, *gora*) means mountain. Livy (XLV. 29. 9) speaks of the "region beyond Bora, the mountain," that is part of what is now old Servia, the region bordering Pela-gonia, whose chief city is now Monastir. There dwelt the Pæonians, a people of Thrako-Illyrian speech. The foot of Bora towards Pieria is sheltered from all Northern blasts.

There grew up the Hyperborean legend, there were the rose-gardens of Midas, and there the "ancient garden of Phœbus."

Apollo was an herbalist, but he has close connection with trees as well as plants. It is still warmly discussed whether the actual name Apollo is derived from the root that gives us *apple* or from *apellon* which means a kind of poplar tree. Setting aside this difficult question, we are on safe ground in asserting that Apollo had close relations to both apple and white poplar tree, but further he was closely connected with the oak of his father, Zeus, and in later days still more closely with the bay-tree, or laurel. Not only at Delphi but as far North as Tempe in Thessaly the laurel was sacred to Apollo. Ælian (*Varia Historia*, III. 1) tells us that Apollo made himself a wreath of the laurel of Tempe and taking in his right hand a branch of this same laurel "came to Delphi and took over the oracle." Here at Delphi for the first time the bay became "prophetic." Apollo was not oracular in Homer as we noted, but he took over the oracular shrine of the old Earth-Goddess, Themis.

What the *Daphnephoria* originally was we learn best not at Delphi, but at Thebes. There, each year and for the space of a year, a boy of distinguished family and himself fair of looks and strong was chosen, Pausanias (IX. 10. 4) tells us, to be the priest of Apollo. To him was given the title of *Daphnephorus*, Laurel-Bearer. A late writer Photius (*Bibliotheca Cod.*, 289), patriarch of Constantinople in the ninth century, has preserved for us details of the ceremony of Laurel-Carrying which are of extraordinary interest. "They wreathe," he says, "a pole of olive wood with laurel and various flowers. On the top is fitted a bronze globe, from which they suspend smaller ones. Midway down the pole they place a smaller globe, binding it with purple fillets,—but the end of the pole is decked with saffron. By the topmost globe they mean the sun, which they actually compare with Apollo. The globe beneath is the moon: the smaller globes hung on are the stars and constellations, and the fillets are the course of the year,— for they make them 365 in number. The *Daphnephorus* himself holds on to the laurel, he has his hair hanging loose, he wears a golden wreath and is dressed out in a splendid robe to his feet and he wears light shoes. There follow him a chorus of maidens, holding out boughs before them to enforce the supplication of the hymns."

The strange ritual implement, half orrery and half maypole, shows plainly as nothing else could how mythology is made and how the godhead mounts from earth to heaven. The maypole first for vegetation, the moon and then the sun, the god as Year Dæmon, and last the young priest, the god in human form;—the ladder from Earth to Heaven is complete.

VIII

❧❧❧❧❧❧❧❧❧❧❧❧❧❧❧❧❧❧❧❧❧❧❧❧❧❧❧❧❧❧❧

Dionysus

The word Dionysus means not "son of Zeus" but rather "Zeus-Young Man," *i.e.*, Zeus in his young form. Dionysus is not so much son of his father, as son of his mother. His mother's name tells us his race. She is Semele, which is only the Thracian form of Zembla, in our *Nova Zembla*, new Earth. Semele is a Thracian and, Thracian, belongs to the so-called *satem* group of languages which turn the guttural into a sibilant,—*se* for *ge*, the Greek for earth. Such languages are in this respect nearer akin to Russian, Persian, Sanskrit, than to Greek, Latin, and Teutonic. Semele is the Thracian Earth-Mother, Dionysus is her son, and on vase-paintings he is figured rising from the earth by her side. He was adopted comparatively late by the Hellenic religion and is always a newcomer to Olympus. Homer barely recognizes his existence.

The figure of Dionysus, like that of Hermes, had humble beginnings. On a beautiful cylix now in Berlin and signed by the master Hieron we have the primitive figure of the god. He is like Hermes, just a rude pillar or post, a tree roughhewn and draped with an embroidered garment. He has a human head. The post is decorated with huge bunches of grapes with sprays of ivy and with great pieces of honeycomb. And round the god's neck is a necklace of dried figs, such as now-a-days a Greek peasant will take with him as provision on a journey. He is clearly the god not of the vine alone but of all natural products. Ivy was much used in his worship and some have seen in the ivy the starting point of the god. About the tree-god, in a great chorus dance his worshippers the Mænads.

Dionysus in the course of his development undoubtedly became the vine-god as well as the ivy-god. But in essence he is something simpler and yet of great significance. He is the god of the ecstasy of the worshipper; he *is* the ecstasy projected. The rapture of the initiated lies essentially in this, as Euripides himself said, that "his soul is congregationalized." It is a group ecstasy. It is this and this only that we desire to emphasize in the figure of Dionysus, it is this that distinguishes him from the other Olympians. The other Olympians are, as we have repeatedly seen, projections of the desires and imaginations—even social conditions—of their worshippers, but it is only in the case of Dionysus that we catch the god at the moment of his making, at the moment when the group ecstasy of the worshipper projects him. Plato (*Phædo*, 69) has preserved for us an Orphic text: "Many are the wand-bearers, but few are the Bacchoi." Many perform the rite of Bacchus, few become or, as we should say, "project" the god himself. Probably all pagan religions went through this stage in which in ecstasy they projected their god, but the Olympians have long passed beyond it. Theirs is the sober service of prayer and praise and sacrifice—God and man are sundered, eternally distinct.

It has been always noted, though till lately never really explained, that Dionysus alone of the Greek gods is always attended by a revel rout of Mænads and Satyrs. Zeus, Athena, Hermes have no such attendants. Dionysus is surrounded by a *thiasos*, that is, by a band of worshippers who project him. Out of the Bacchoi emerges Bacchus. But at this point it will rightly be asked how could a company of Mænads, young women, project the figure of a young male god? They could not and they did not. The Satyrs project Dionysus, but the Mænads project the figure of the Mother. The worship of Dionysus is always dual, of mother and son, though in later poetry the mother sometimes appears as nurse. Thus Sophocles, in the *Œdipus at Colonus* (679):

Footless, sacred, shadowy thicket, where a myriad berries grow,
Where no heat of the sun may enter, neither wind of the winter
    blow,
Where the Reveller Dionysos with his Nursing Nymphs will go.

The Bacchants are the Mothers and theirs is the magical power to make the whole world break into blossom; they tend the young of the wild things.

And one a young fawn held, and one a wild
Wolf cub, and fed them with white milk, and smiled
In love, young mothers with a mother's breast
And babes at home forgotten!

On Mt. Cithæron all creation stirs anew to life at the great ritual of the Mothers:

And all the mountain felt,
And worshipped with them; and the wild things knelt
And ramped and gloried, and the wilderness
Was filled with moving voices and dim stress.[45]

Such are the moments when the gods are made.

IX

Zeus

We have left Zeus to the end mainly because his figure is not only supreme but in one way different from that of the other Olympians. He is more elemental, there is in him more of the thing worshipped and less of the worshipper. His "element" is quite clearly and avowedly the sky, the upper air. When the gods divided all things into three lots, Homer (*Il.*, XV. 187 ff.) tells us Poseidon drew the sea, Hades the murky darkness, and Zeus "the wide heaven." In his monumental work *Zeus, the European Sky-God*, Mr. A. B. Cook has shown that Zeus *is* the Sky in its two aspects, the Bright Sky to which belong the æther, the Sun, and Moon, and every shining constellation, the Dark Sky with the thunder, the storm cloud, and the rain. So in Homer, Zeus is before all things the Loud-Thunderer, the Cloud-Gatherer, "he lighteneth, fashioning either a mighty rain unspeakable, or hail, or snow, when the flakes sprinkle all the ploughed lands." [46] His messenger is Iris, the Rainbow.

The human Zeus of Homer scarcely commands admiration; he is shamelessly licentious, he bullies and even maltreats his wife; when his will is crossed, he is apt to behave like an uncontrolled thunderstorm; but there are beginnings of higher things, specially in the kindly aspect of Zeus as God of

Strangers, suppliants and even beggars. It is, however, to the profoundly religious Æschylus that we mainly owe the moralizing of the character of Zeus. Zeus was to him, through faith, the solution of all world problems: "Zeus, Power Unknown, whom, since so to be called is his pleasure, I so address. When I ponder upon all things, I can conjecture naught but 'Zeus,' to fit the need, if the burden of vanity is in very truth to be cast from the soul." (Æsch., *Agamemnon*, 160 ff.) "Never, never shall mortal counsels outpass the Harmony of Zeus" (Æsch., *Prometheus Bound*, 551).

It happens very fortunately that Phidias in his great chryselephantine statue of Zeus embodied the ideals of the age of Æschylus, and still more fortunately some of the impressions are recorded of the spectators of the statue. Quintilian (XII. 10. 9) said of the Olympian Zeus that "its beauty seemed to have added something to revealed religion." Dio Chrysostom (XII. 14) wrote: "our Zeus is peaceful and altogether mild, as the guardian of Hellas when she is of one mind and not distraught with faction, an image gentle and august in perfect form, one who is the giver of life and breath and every good gift, the 'common father and saviour and guardian of mankind'"—so far as it was possible for a mortal to conceive and embody a nature infinite and divine. The image brought to the troubled heart of the beholder something of its own large repose, for, "if there be any of mortals whatsoever that is heavy-laden in spirit, having suffered sorely many sorrows and calamities in his life, nor yet winning for himself sweet sleep, even such an one, methinks, standing before the image of the god, would forget all things whatsoever in his mortal life were hard to be endured, so wondrously hast thou, Phidias, conceived and wrought it and such grace and light shine upon it from thine art."

Conclusion

It is fitting that our argument should end with the great plastic image of Zeus, for this brings us to the very core or kernel of our debt to Greek mythology. This debt is two-fold. We owe to Greek mythology, first, the heritage of a matchless imagery, an imagery which has haunted the minds of poets and artists down to the present day, second, a thing, as we shall see, intimately connected with this imagery, the release of the human spirit in part at least from the baneful obsession of fear.

First as to the heritage of imagery. Let us say at once that the debt is spiritual and not to be measured by definite borrowings. The modern poet or artist does not adopt a Greek myth as we may take over a bit of Roman Law, or a definite discovery in mathematics, or some abstract conception in Greek philosophy. It would indeed be easy—and exceedingly tedious—to note and tabulate how often Shakespeare or Milton or Keats or Tennyson have suddenly illuminated their verse by a "classical allusion." It is harder, but more profitable, to ask that these "classical allusions," these mythological images and myths, have this magical power of illumination.

The effect of Greek imagery on a poet's mind probably defies ultimate analysis, but this much may be said. An image is a thing widely different from an abstraction. It is not in any sense even a collection of qualities abstracted and recombined for purposes of religious edification. A nation less gifted loads the name of its god with epithets and his idol with attributes; the Greek, because dowered with imagination, *feels* his god as a *personality*, with a live human history. This god is as much the outcome of his emotions as of his intellect —perhaps even more. The life of the Greek people is re-lived in him. It is because of this great *actuality* of the Greek gods that we have been at pains to show in detail how they came to be, how they express and project the life of the people who imagined them.

But reality in godhead, though it is much, though it lends to the divine figures a warmth and solidity and gladness that cheers and supports, is not enough. For a god to be really a god, he and his myth must touch us with some remote and magical appeal, something of light supernal and grace unspeakable, something that gives release from the ever imminent actual. It is, I think, through this blend of the real and the unreal that the gods and myths of the Greeks remain perennially potent in literature, while the mythical monstrosities of Egypt, Assyria, and India are doomed to a sterile death.

The second factor in our debt to Greek mythology is perhaps not greater, but simpler and much more easy to formulate. It is that from religion Greek mythology banished fear, fear which poisons and paralyzes man's life.

"Who is there," asks the Roman poet, Lucretius, "whose mind does not shrink into itself with fear of the gods?" [47]

Praeterea cui non animus formidine divum Contrahitur?
One people, one only, the Greeks. To them religion was a thing of glad confidence, of high fellowship with the gods. Some *rites* of fear and repulsion they kept, for ritual is always

conservative, but their mythology and theology, in their *representations* of the gods, was informed throughout by reason, lighted by beauty; it was a thing, as they themselves would say, of *sophrosyne*, of sane thinking and feeling.

How was fear banished? By the making of beautiful images. The first gift of the Greek genius brought inevitably in its train the second. This connection is to us of supreme interest and of no small psychological importance. By some inspired instinct, the Greek seems to have anticipated in practice the latest discoveries in modern psychology and especially in modern therapeutics. To banish fear, to banish any evil, we must exercise not the will but the imagination, we must not so much determine to be brave, not make "good resolutions," but *think* brave, cheering thoughts, think good things, beautiful things. Plato desired for the young citizens of his ideal Republic that they should "pasture" their minds on beautiful thoughts. In a word, according to the new psychology of Coué, Baudouin, and a host of disciples, if will and imagination conflict, it is imagination that comes off victor. Thought, imagination is the starting point of action. And above all, let that thought be active, live, positive, not negative. As Baudouin[48] has well said: *"Veni Creator* is in all ways a much surer method of exorcism than *Vade retro Satanas."* As a Greek would think it, it is better to domicile the Eumenides than to expel the Erinyes.

The religious influence of the Olympian gods, mild, serene, beautiful, has been incalculable. Touched by their humanity, the Hebrew Jehovah lost much of his savagery, many of the traits he owes to the irresponsible thunderstorm. When in the Middle Ages Greek civilization and with it the figures of the Greek gods suffered eclipse, the banished ghosts of superstition came flocking back, man is hag-ridden by fear and fear engenders savagery; the Inquisition is the logical outcome of a terror-stricken conscience. His terrors can only be abated by a Renaissance, a rebirth of the old Greek habit of thinking in calm, beautiful imagery. Each generation has its own terrors; we are now not panic-stricken by the pains of Hell, we shiver instead before the perils of heredity, the hidden germ, the broken nerve, the insistent *phobia*. We still need to think Greek thoughts and feed our souls upon Greek imagery. Ruskin has told us why we need the Greeks:

"There is no dread in their hearts; pensiveness, amazement, often deepest grief and desolation, but terror never. Everlasting calm in the presence of all fate, and joy such as they might win, not indeed from perfect beauty but from beauty at perfect rest."

Notes

꒱꒱

1. *Odyssey*, V. 43-55, translation by J. W. Mackail.
2. *Odyssey*, X. 275-280 and 302-306, translation by J. W. Mackail, London and New York.
3. *Odyssey*, XXIV. 1-12, translation by S. H. Butcher and A. Lang, London and New York, 1900.
4. Shakespeare, *Hamlet*, III. 459.
5. Aristophanes, *Knights*, 550.
6. Sophocles, *Œdipus at Colonus*, 700 ff., translation by D. S. MacColl. (Made for me.)
7. Festus, *De significatione verborum*, 101, "Hippius."
8. Euripides, *Hippolytus*, 1201 ff., translation by Gilbert Murray, London, 1906.
9. Sophocles, *Trachiniæ*, 9 ff., translation by J. E. H.
10. *Odyssey*, IX. 275 ff., and 524, translation by J. W. Mackail.
11. Euripides, *Electra*, 458 ff., translation by Gilbert Murray, London, 1912.
12. Euripides, *Trojan Women*, 511 ff., translation by Gilbert Murray, London, 912.
13. *Odyssey*, III. 3 ff., and 55 ff., translations by J. W. Mackail.
14. Euripides, *Bacchæ*, 130 ff., translation by Gilbert Murray, London, 1906. See n. 8.
15. Hesiod, *Works and Days*, 69 ff., translation by D. S. MacColl. (Made for me.)
16. *Odyssey*, IX. 633 ff., translation by J. E. H.

17. Aeschylus, *Eumenides*, 46 ff., translation by J. E. H.

18. Aeschylus, *Eumenides*, 903 ff. and 938 ff., translations by D. S. MacColl. (Made for me.)

19. *Paradise Lost*, IV. 269 ff.

19ᵃ. Shakespeare, *The Winter's Tale*, IV. 4, 116.

20. Swinburne, *Hymn to Proserpine*.

21. Swinburne, *The Garden of Proserpine*.

22. Matthew Arnold, *Thyrsis*.

23. Homeric *Hymn to Demeter*, translations by J. E. H.

24. Tennyson, *Demeter, and Persephone*.

25. Theocritus, *Idylls*, VII. 155, translation by J. E. H.

26. Tennyson, *Oenone*.

27. *Odyssey*, XX. 67 ff., translation by J. E. H.

28. Sophocles, *Oedipus at Colonus*, 700 ff., translation by D. S. MacColl. (Made for me.)

29. Swinburne, *Erechtheus*.

30. Swinburne, *Atalanta in Calydon*.

31. Lucretius, *De Aerum Natura*, I, 1 ff., translation by J. E. H.

32. *Homeric Hymn*, VI. 2, translation by Gilbert Murray. (Made for me.)

33. Theognis, 1275-9, translation by J. E. H.

34. Sophocles, *Antigone*, 781 ff., translation by Gilbert Murray. (Made for me.)

35. Euripides, *Hippolytus*, translation by Gilbert Murray.

36. Euripides, *Iphigenia in Tauris*, translations by Gilbert Murray, London, 1911.

37. Swinburne, *Atalanta in Calydon*.

38. *Odyssey*, XV. 407 ff., translation by J. W. Mackail.

39. Browning, *Caliban upon Setebos*.

40. Theocritus, *Idylls*, II. 18 ff., translation by J. E. H.

41. Euripides, *Hippolytus*, translations by Gilbert Murray.

42. *Anthologia Palatina*, or, *The Greek Anthology*, VI. 280, translation by J. E. H.

43. Euripides, *Hippolytus*, translation by W. H. Mallock, London, 1906.

44. "The Connection of Paean with Paeonia," in *The Classical Review*, XXVI. 249 (1912).

45. Euripides, *Bacchæ*, 726 ff., translations by Gilbert Murray.
46. *Iliad*, X. 5 ff., translation by Lang, Leaf and Myers, London and New York, 1900.
47. Lucretius, *De Rerum Natura*, V. 1218, translation by H. A. J. Munro, Cambridge, England, 1891.
48. Charles Baudouin, *Suggestion et Autosuggestion*, Paris, p. 153, translation by E. and C. Paul, New York, 1921.

Bibliography

COOK, A. B., *Zeus, A Study in Ancient Religion.* Cambridge, England, 1914.

D'OOGE, B. L., *Helps to the Study of Classical Mythology.* Ann Arbor, Michigan, 1899.

EVANS, ARTHUR J., *Mycenaean Tree and Pillar Cult.* London and New York, 1901.

—————, *The Palace of Minos.* London and New York, 1921.

FAIRBANKS, ARTHUR, *A Handbook of Greek Religion.* New York, 1910.

—————, *The Mythology of Greece and Rome* (presented with special reference to its influence on literature). New York, 1907.

FARNELL, L. R., *The Cults of the Greek States.* 5 vols. Oxford, 1896-1909.

FRAZER, J. G., *The Golden Bough,* a Study in Magic and Religion. 1 vol. London and New York, 1923.

—————, *Apollodorus, The Library, with an English Translation,* in *The Loeb Classical Library.* 2 vols. London and New York, 1921.

FOX, WM. SHERWOOD, *Greek and Roman Mythology,* in *The Mythology of all Races.* Boston, 1916. (Full bibliography.)

GAYLEY, C. M., *The Classic Myths in English Literature and in*

GRUPPE, O., *Griechische Mythologie und Religionsgeschichte*, in Ivan von Müller's *Handbuch der Klassischen Altertumswissenschaft*. V. 2. 1. and 2. Munich, 1906.

GUERBER, H. A., *Myths of Greece and Rome* (narrated with special reference to literature and art). New York, 1893.

HARRINGTON, K. P., and TOLMAN, H. C., *Greek and Roman Mythology*. Boston, 1897.

HARRIS, JAMES RENDEL, *The Ascent of Olympus*. Manchester, 1917.

HARRISON, JANE ELLEN, *Prolegomena to the Study of Greek Religion*.² Cambridge, England, 1908.

——————, *Themis, A Study of the Social Origins of Greek Religion*. Cambridge, England, 1912.

——————, *Epilegomena to the Study of Greek Religion*. Cambridge, England, 1921.

——————, *Ancient Art and Ritual*, in *The Home University Library*. New York and London, 1913.

——————, *The Religion of Ancient Greece*, in *Religions, Ancient and Modern*. London and Chicago, 1905.

LEUBA, JAMES H., *The Psychological Origin and the Nature of Religion*, in *Religions, Ancient and Modern*. London and Chicago, 1909.

MURRAY, GILBERT, *Four Stages of Greek Religion*. New York, 1912.

OSGOOD, CHARLES G., *The Classical Mythology of Milton's English Poems*. New York, 1900.

ROBERT, KARL, and PRELLER, LUDWIG, *Griechische Mythologie*.⁴ Berlin, 1894-1921.

ROSCHER, W. H., *Ausführliches Lexikon der Griechischen und Römischen Mythologie*. Leipzig, 1885 ff. Supplement: *Geschichte der klassischen Mythologie und Religionsgeschichte während des Mittelalters im Abendland und während der Neuzeit*. Von Otto Gruppe, 1921.